America's Retirement Plan

An Employer's Guide to Understanding the 401(k) Plan

Robert H. Gorelick, APA

 www.trafford.com

North America & international
toll-free: 1 888 232 4444 (USA & Canada)
phone: 250 383 6864 • fax: 250 383 6804 • email: info@trafford.com

The United Kingdom & Europe
phone: +44 (0)1865 722 113 • local rate: 0845 230 9601
facsimile: +44 (0)1865 722 868 • email: info.uk@trafford.com

10 9 8 7 6 5 4 3 2

Table of Contents

Acknowledgements

First and foremost I want to thank my wife, Wendy ,
my daughter Carrie and my daughter and son-in-law Susan and Mark Russell,
for their support and encouragement.

Thank you to:
The law firm of *Reish Luftman Reicher & Cohen* for their research into
fiduciary obligations. Most of the comments about fiduciary liability
in this book stem from their hands-on knowledge and discussions
with the Internal Revenue Service and the Department of Labor.

Nationwide Financial for their sample Investment Policy Statement
and Fiduciary Checklist.

The staff at Benefit Equity Inc. for their support and input.

Kory Ngo for his explanation of Penmax, the combination defined
benefit and defined contribution plan design.

Ian Crockett, Bethany Van Mill and Karen Todd
for their editing and valuable input.

Introduction

THE KEY TO EMPLOYEES ACHIEVING SUCCESSFUL RETIREMENT SAVINGS LIES WITH THEIR EMPLOYER. Individual retirement accounts (IRAs) have proven to be inadequate. The best system to help the American worker achieve retirement savings is the 401(k) plan. Even with this great saving plan Americans are asking themselves whether they will have enough money to retire.

The 2006 Retirement Confidence Survey* found that the percentage of workers who are very confident about having enough money to live comfortably in retirement is a paltry 24% and that figure has been basically stable since 1998. Only 44% of workers who have not saved for retirement feel confident they will have enough money to live comfortably in retirement. If we look at the amount of reported savings and investments (not counting primary residence or defined benefit plans), 53% of all workers have saved less than $25,000 and only 12% have more than $25,000.

Only 40% of workers think they need to accumulate at least $500,000 by the time they retire to live comfortably in retirement. Twenty percent think they will

---

* Employee Benefit Research Institute and Mathew Greenwald & Associates, Inc.

need between $250,000 and $499,999, and 30% think they need to save less than $250,000 for a comfortable retirement.

American workers do not realize how much income it takes to maintain their pre-retirement standard of living. Half think they can have a comfortable retirement with less than 70% of their pre-retirement income, and nearly 30% believe they will be comfortable with 70 to 85 percent.

When current retirees are surveyed, more than half have income that is the same or better than their pre-retirement income. Financial planners suggest that workers should plan to replace at least 70% of their pre-retirement income.

Workers must save more and be given more education about how much it will take to retire comfortably. The vehicle to take us there is the 401(k) plan, which has become the number one savings plan for American workers preparing for retirement.

401(k) plans are taking the place of traditional pension plans called "defined benefit plans." However, the problem with 401(k) plans (compared to defined benefit plan pension plans) is that only 65% to 75% of employees participate in their company's 401(k) plan.

This situation worries Congress. If the nation is moving away from company-sponsored pension plans covering all employees to a voluntary system, many workers may end up with only social security benefits. Therefore, we will continue to see Congress pass laws to encourage retirement savings.

There are many different government-approved retirement plans, but the 401(k) plan is the retirement plan of choice of most successful businesses. However, businesses need help understanding the complex concepts and issues that arise from these plans.

The complexity is mainly due to Congress putting laws on the books to prevent employers from creating plans that only benefit themselves or a select few. There are laws to penalize those who cheat. Cheating occurs when employers use the money in the plan for their own benefit. Although not very common employers have used the money they or their employees have contributed to the plan for their own benefit.

The law that forms the framework for retirement plans is known as the Employee Retirement Income Security Act of 1974 (ERISA). ERISA is the most comprehensive law regarding benefits ever written. ERISA has been amended (changed) almost every other year since 1974 and contains a complex set of rules designed primarily to provide security for the average worker and limit the amount of benefits for the wealthy. ERISA contains the rules we must play by.

The latest law to amend ERISA is the Pension Protection Act, passed in August, 2006. This law approved an enrollment process, called "automatic enrollment." In this plan, employers can automatically enroll employees for anywhere from 3% to 10% of their pay. Congress sees this as a way to obtain full participation in 401(k) plans.

Employee money is safer today than ever due to ERISA and an industry of professional retirement plan consultants and administrators, who help employers manage 401(k) plans. These people are known as "third party administrators" (TPA's). They handle everything from designing a plan to fit your company to keeping you out of trouble with the government. They work for a fee, similar to how you pay your accountant or attorney for services.

A TPA helps you abide by the abundance of rules and regulations governing retirement plans. If you do not comply with the rules (i.e., ERISA) you can lose the tax deductibility and tax-deferred growth that make these plans both popular and affordable.

This is where I come in. I'm a TPA. My job is to help employers manage these plans and keep themselves out of trouble with the government. Most financial institutions selling 401(k) plans recognize there is considerable complexity to the plans and package the 401(k) plan so neatly that employers are mostly unaware of what they need to know to maintain these programs. This eventually gets the employer in trouble. (See Chapter VI on Fiduciary Responsibility to get an idea of the liability involved when sponsoring a retirement plan.)

Retirement plans such as the 401(k) have a language of their own, which I call "pensionese." If you are not familiar with the language, you will not fully comprehend your advisors and overlook details that will cost your staff time and cost you money. You will also find yourself with more liability and exposure than you ever thought possible.

Although not a technical reference, this book will give decision-makers such as business owners, company officers and HR Managers the insight they need into the complex world of retirement plans. It will also help financial advisors understand some of the administrative aspects of the 401(k) plan. It is designed to meet the needs of medium-to-small-size businesses (as opposed to very large corporations).

Although I believe our government will do whatever is necessary to maintain the Social Security system, it will not be enough without personal savings.

I believe the employer is the best delivery system to assist employees with long-term savings and that the 401(k) plan can do the best job helping workers obtain retirement security.

The government has written approximately *4000 pages* of rules and regulations on retirement plans! I will cut this overwhelming amount of information down to a little over 100 pages. (The very thought of my simplifying this subject will have pension actuaries rolling their eyes and writing to the publisher to remove the book from store shelves!)

The 401(k) is becoming America's Retirement Plan. However, we must be careful. Unless employers of all sizes embrace the 401(k) as a core benefit, our government will impose it — or something like it — on us. Do you want to be in control of your benefits or do you want the government to impose a retirement plan on you? Hopefully the insight you get from this book will arm you with the information to understand the importance of this retirement plan for you and your employees.

1

The 401(k) Plan

Overview

Corporations have been offering employee savings plans to their employees since the 1950s. Back then, they were called Cash or Deferral Arrangements. The Revenue Act of 1978 created section 401(k) of the Internal Revenue Code (IRS) and so the name "401(k) Plan" was coined. It was not until 1981, however, that the IRS proposed regulations for 401(k) plans. (Without government regulations or rules, employers can never be sure they won't run afoul of the law.) After the regulations were put in place in 1981, benefit plan consultants and financial advisors began recommending this new plan to corporations.

By 1986, 401(k) plans were being widely used by large corporations. However, it was not until the early 1990s that 401(k)'s become popular with small-to-medium-size companies. Today almost all large companies have 401(k) plans while a little over 50% of small-to-medium-size companies have these plans.

A 401(k) plan allows employees working for a business that sponsors a plan to save money from their paycheck *pre-tax* and invest it on a *tax-deferred* basis. The money is invested in mutual funds or similar investments. (See Chapter VIII on Investments for more information.)

Most companies have an eligibility period or waiting period before an employee can enroll in the plan. After completing the eligibility period, money is taken from the employee's paycheck and invested. Some companies automatically enroll their employees in the plan and others require action by the individual employee to enroll. In either case, enrollment is voluntary. Once an employee enrolls in the plan, they can save up to $15,500 (periodically adjusted for the cost of living) per year plus another $5000 (called "catch-up"), if the employee is 50 or older. When the money is distributed or paid to the employee, taxes are due. (I tell employees to think of this money as their paycheck when they stop working or retire.)

Employers have the discretion to match employee contributions or to contribute to all eligible employees. The contribution amount or formula is determined based on the employer's pocketbook. Many employers come up with their own formula based on what other employers in their industry contribute to these plans.

Six Reasons Employers Offer a 401(k) Plan

The main reasons companies offer 401(k) plans are that they:
  1 Help employees save money for retirement
  2 Help retain good employees
  3 Provide a competitive edge when hiring
  4 Allow employees to choose and control their investments
  5 Supplement or replace a Defined Benefit Pension Plan

In addition:
  6 Contributions to the plan are tax deductible.

In today's competitive job environment, companies that do not have a good 401(k) plan are at a hiring disadvantage.

There are two primary reasons companies do not have a 401(k) Plan: (1) They feel it is too expensive and/or (2) employees' do not participate.

Reverse Discrimination

Any size employer can have a 401(k) plan. The only limitation is that you cannot set the plan up so only the executives or owners benefit if you have other employees. The government has a series of nondiscrimination tests to be sure the highest-paid employees (called the "highly compensated employees" [HCE's]) are not getting all the benefits.

The HCE's may be limited by what they can save if all other employees (referred to as "non-highly compensated employees" [NHCE's]) either do not save or do not save enough. This is actually reverse discrimination. The maximum savings limit is $15,500 for 2007. However, HCE's are limited in how much they can defer when NHCE's don't save or save enough.

There is a non-discrimination test which is performed annually to limit what the HCE's can defer. For example, if the average savings rate for all the NHCE's is 4% of pay, then the most the HCE's can save on average is 6% of pay. Generally, HCE's can save only 2% of their pay more than the average of what all other eligible employees save. This means that if employees do not save very much, the highest-paid employees will be limited in how much they can save. (For more detailed information about HCE's, NHCE's and nondiscrimination testing, see Chapter VII on Plan Design.)

One reason 401k plans do not live up to the executive's savings expectations is lack of education for their staff. If employees are not well informed about the plan they don't participate.

The two important components that make a 401(k) plan successful are
employee education and investment advice.

Survey of 401(k) Plans

Knowing what others are doing with 401(k) plans allows you to make better decisions. Here are some statistics for you to use to see how your plan measures up.

According to a survey by *Plan Sponsor Magazine* of 4741 plans of all sizes (November 2005):

- The average plan participation by employees is 75%.
- The median employee deferral is 6% of pay.
- The average number of investment options in a plan is 18.

- The average number of investments held by participants is 5.
- Matching is offered by 77.5% of employers.
- Matching formulas:
- 31% offered a match of 50% up to 6% deferred.
- 34% offered more than 50% of 6% deferred.
- 35% offered less than 50% of 6% deferred.

(Note: 50% up to 6% means if you save 6% or more of salary your employer will give you half [50%] of 6% or 3% of your salary.)
- 71% had an Investment Policy Statement.
- 14% had automatic enrollment.*
- 47% had automatic rebalancing.
- Waiting Period to enter plan:
- 32% had no eligibility period.
- 24% had 3 months or less.
- 11% had 6 months or less.
- 33% had 6 months or more.

Ten Roles and Responsibilities

Employers, recognizing they lack the knowledge necessary to manage 401(k) plans, outsource their plan to professionals. The retirement plan industry has investment companies, benefits companies, actuaries, accountants, lawyers, third party administrators, banks, and trust companies all providing services to 401(k) sponsors (employers). As a group, providers of retirement plan services are referred to as "providers."

Here is a summary of their roles and responsibilities.
1 plan design and consulting
2 investments
3 record keeping for the investments
4 benefit statements for participants
5 legal plan documentation
6 government compliance tests
7 distributions to terminated participants

---

* The Pension Protection Act of 2006 has made automatic enrollment a preferred option in plan design. Participation rates are 22% higher with plans offering automatic enrollment.

8 enrollment assistance

9 employee education, and

10 annual report/return Form 5500.

Determining the best provider(s) for your company can be challenging. As you delve into it, you will find that a 401(k) plan is conceptually straightforward but laden with complexity. Understanding investments and government compliance requirements is not what you are trained to do.

What most people do not realize is that, more often than not, providers do only the minimum required and avoid taking on any fiduciary responsibility. Read their service agreement and you will find that it says the *employer* is the "responsible party." Some providers say they will be a "co-fiduciary" with you, but that still does not alleviate you from liability.

Investment providers that sell inexpensive packaged plans will keep track of your money but are not responsible for plan compliance details required by law. They usually prepare reports that tell you if you pass some of the compliance tests and may even complete reports and tax returns the government requires. However, they seldom give advice or take on any liability for the compliance aspects of the plan.

It says right on the government's tax return for the plan (Form 5500) that the business owner or company officer is signing under penalty of perjury that the information on the return is true and correct, but how would you know if the information on the form you are signing is true and correct? With the advent of electronic filing of tax returns, do you review what the provider has given to the government on your behalf? (They are required to send you a copy that you sign and retain.)

If you have a plan subject to independent audit, it is likely the auditor will find any problems that may have occurred during the year. However, if you have less than 100 participants (the threshold for an audit), you may not find out there are inconsistencies until the government audits it, and then it too late to fix the problem without incurring penalties.

Therefore it makes sense to deal with a retirement plan consultant who *specializes in retirement plans* to guide you and be *your trusted advisor*.

Plan Administration

Most of the organizations selling 401(k) plans rarely go into detail on all the responsibilities you are on the hook for until after you bought their plan. After all, most of the time you are talking to a sales representative.

The best providers will spend time with you or your staff going over what they do and what is expected of you, but they are talking in "pensionese," the language of retirement plans. When they are all done talking, it either feels as if you did not get enough information to make an educated decision or you just feel dumb.

Although there are many 401(k)'s operating today, how the plan operates (otherwise referred to as "plan administration") remains a mystery to small and mid-size employers. Large corporations have benefit departments, but still use outside consultants to keep them out of trouble.

To understand a 401(k) plan, you need to know that there are *six key elements* to it.

Obtaining knowledge about these six key areas will help you judge whether you have a good provider. It will also provide you with the guidelines for managing the ongoing process of sponsoring a 401(k) plan.

The Six Key Elements of a 401(k) Plan

There are six elements to a 401(k) Plan:

1 **Fiduciary Responsibility**: This standard mandates prudent management and oversight of a qualified retirement plan.
2 **Plan Document**: This is a legal document (generally known as the "plan and trust document") which describes how the plan will operate. It contains the plan design, operational guidelines and government rules.
3 **Administration**: This is the job of the Third Party Administrator (TPA) (also known as a "professional plan administrator") hired to manage all the rules set forth in the plan document. The insurance company or investment company that you hire may offer this service, too.
4 **Recordkeeping***: The record keeper receives a check from the employer each pay period and invests it according to the trustee's direction or the participant's direction. This is a job completed for you by the investment company,

---

*   All mutual fund investments or trades must be "cleared" or settled. This process is the buying and selling of securities or moving money from one mutual fund to another.

trust company or TPA.

5 **Investments**: Most plans allow their plan participants to invest their money in mutual funds. Mutual funds are purchased from 401(k) investment providers such as insurance companies, stock brokerages or directly from the mutual fund. The organization you purchase your mutual funds/investments through is usually the record keeper, too.

6 **Education**: Enrollment brochures provide information about the plan and the investment offerings. Additional information is available online and through on-sight meetings held by the investment company and/or financial advisor.

The following is a more detailed explanation of these elements. As you progress through the book, you will receive more insight on the interplay between these elements.

Fiduciary Responsibility

Any person who exercises discretion or control over the management of the plan or its assets or who is paid to give investment advice regarding plan assets is a *fiduciary*. The duties a person performs for the plan, rather than his or her title, or office, determines whether that person is a plan fiduciary. Plan fiduciaries generally include the business owners, plan trustees, Registered Investment Advisors (RIA) and members of a plan's investment committee. Providers such as actuaries, accountants, brokers, professional plan administrators and record keepers are not fiduciaries unless they exercise discretion or are responsible for the management of the plan or its assets. (ERISA Section 3(21); DOL Regulation Section 2509.75-8, D-2)

> *A fiduciary is a person who occupies a position of such power and confidence with regard to the property of another that the law requires him to act solely in the interest of the person whom he represents.*

This is the highest standard of law relating to responsibility for money and property.

Plan Document

An Employer who sponsors a retirement plan must adopt and maintain a legal plan document. This document is the manual that sets forth how the plan will operate. This plan document must be kept up-to-date with all the government's rules and regulations.

You do not have a legal 401(k) or other qualified retirement plan without a plan document. (See Chapter XI on The Plan Document for more detail.)

Administration

The government has a set of rules you must follow to keep your plan qualified. The standard for small-to-medium-size employers is to outsource the compliance components of the plan.

The people schooled in retirement plan rules are called plan consultants, actuaries, third party administrators, attorneys and accountants. These people make great efforts to be known in their communities and have impressive credentials, and they have no qualms about reciting the rules to you and insisting you follow them.

If you do not follow the rules, the plan can be disqualified and you can be heavily fined. The reason plan providers are strict about following the rules is that they can become liable if they know you are not following the rules.

Compliance entails being sure participants do not exceed contribution limits and do not enter the plan too early or, for that matter, too late. There are non-discrimination tests called ADP and ACP tests along with coverage tests, participation tests, top heavy testing, cross testing…and the list goes on. The relevance of these tests depends upon your plan design. The point I want to make is that without good third party administrative support your staff must take on more work and be more knowledgeable.

I suggest you hire a professional plan administrator known as a third party administrator (TPA), as opposed to having one imposed on you by a "bundled" provider (i.e., a company which handles everything).

The government takes compliance very seriously! Their rules are both complex and daunting. You cannot use the excuse, "I didn't know," because the rules are all in writing and published by the government. Therefore, you should hire a professional to assist you in carrying out the terms of the plan. It does not matter how good your investments are or how engaging the enrollments materials are if you violate the terms of the plan.

Recordkeeping

Every time payroll is paid, employees participating in the plan are required to have their 401(k) deferral sent to the record keeper. Also, when a participant wants to change the way they have invested their money, they go online to the record keeper's web site. The Internet is the prescribed way for a participant to move their money from one mutual fund to another: they can monitor their investments and get all kinds of education and supporting documentation there.

The record keeper can be an investment company, a mutual fund group, an insurance company, bank, trust company or a third party administrator.

Investments

It is the job of the Trustee, who is usually also the business owner, to hire the investment provider. The investment provider can be any organization licensed to sell investments. The trustee is responsible for the money and makes the decisions on how the money will be invested. Since the business owner is usually the trustee, the business owner is in effect the responsible party.

Most 401(k) plans are designed to conform to Department of Labor Regulation 404(c) and pass the responsibility for investing the money from the trustee to the plan participant. This is called a self-directed plan. However, *it is the trustee's job to decide what investments will be made available for the plan participants.*

Plan investments should be reviewed quarterly and measured against appropriate benchmarks. A report is generated annually indicating how the investments performed over one, three and five years. Some providers do this automatically for you. If all they do is provide a list of mutual funds, you should hire an investment advisor to help you review the funds.

Education

The standard for education of employees for small employers is a company meeting conducted by the investment advisor. These meetings explain the plan provisions, how much they should save for retirement, and information about the investments. (See Chapter VIII on Investments and Chapter IX on Employee Education for more information on what to expect from an employee meeting.)

Summary

- Fiduciary responsibility,
- Plan documentation,
- Administrative compliance,
- Keeping track of the money in participant accounts,
- Investment best practices and
- Employee education

are the rudimentary aspects of any 401(k) plan.

Failure to understand how the six elements work together is the main reason employers become disenchanted with their 401(k) plan.

In the next chapter, I will explore in more detail areas to be familiar with when establishing a 401(k) plan.

2

The 401(k) Plan Part II

KNOWING ABOUT THE SIX ELEMENTS (DISCUSSED IN CHAPTER 1) IS IMPORTANT, BUT IT IS JUST AS IMPORTANT TO UNDERSTAND HOW THEY WORK TOGETHER. The following discusses all but the education element (which is presented in the chapters on Employee Education and Investments).

You are Responsible!

A 401(k) plan must be in writing. 401(k) programs must have *both a plan document and an investment contract*. For example, when signing up with a provider such as a mutual fund company or insurance company, you may only get an investment contract, not the legal plan documentation (Plan & Trust), indicating you have a qualified retirement plan.

It is important for you to know the difference between a "plan document" and an "investment contract." It is also prudent to have an attorney or qualified TPA review what you are buying. Do not trust the investment company sales representative on issues of legal documentation — this is not their area of expertise. Think of a 401(k) plan as a company or business and the investments as its product.

I have seen many employers who have not signed a plan document invest their money and their employees' money with an investment company. However, according to the law, they do not have a 401(k) plan. This means all the money is *taxable* and all tax deductions were *illegal*! *You* are the fiduciary and liable for the plan's operation and investments.

The way people who sell 401(k) plans soften your liability and diminish their own liability is to promote DOL regulation known as 404(c). This ruling sets forth nineteen requirements that, if followed, protect plan sponsors (employers) from being sued for poor investment decisions made by the plan participants. However, it does not protect the employer if the employer fails to select good investments or fails to monitor and remove poor-performing investments.

It is widely known that most employees have never invested money before entering a 401(k) plan and admit to knowing little if anything about investments. Too many employers assume that their plans comply with Department of Labor Regulation 404(c) and put their employees into these plans believing that they are "off the hook" if participants do not invest wisely. However, I find that most employers do not understand that the law *makes them responsible* for having appropriate investments, regardless of whether they follow provisions under regulation 404(c).

"Employer's who set up the plans are responsible for choosing the correct investments to be offered to their employees."

(DEPT OF LABOR REGULATION SECTION 2550.404A-1(B)(2))

Revenue Sharing

Record keepers make money by both charging the mutual funds for doing supporting services (revenue sharing) and, to the extent that they do not receive enough to make a profit, charge the balance to your plan in the form of a fee, also known as an "asset management fee" (which is usually paid for by the participants).

Money for support services (called "revenue sharing") has become a point of contention because people concerned about plan expenses see this as an area of non-disclosure that affects plan participants. Both insurance companies and stock brokerages collect fees for supporting services they provide. These revenue sharing payments are in addition to the sales charges, annual distribution and service fees that are disclosed in the fund's prospectus. It should be noted that these revenue sharing payments are paid out of the investment adviser's or fund affiliate's revenues and not from the fund's assets. However, revenue from affiliated entities may be derived from fees earned for services provided to and paid for by the fund.

To summarize, revenue sharing generally does not cost the investor more. However, you should know if your provider is getting revenue from mutual funds because if they push funds with revenue sharing over others you have a fiduciary obligation to be sure those funds have reasonable fees and perform as good as others offered. (I will discuss what a plan costs in Chapter IV, The Right Plan.)

The Right Investments

Several studies show too few investment choices reduce a participant's ability to make money and too many confuse an employee and lead to either apathy or poor choice of investment alternatives.[*]

In addition to the right mix of investments, if you know your employees are not well educated when it comes to investing and you do not offer an investment advisor, you should provide portfolios of diversified investments based on risk, age and time to retirement. (See Chapter VIII on Investments for examples of portfolios.)

Many employers offer investment advice, and advice comes in several forms. The most popular is one-on-one consultation between advisor and participant, and then online advice and newsletters, all of which require that the participant take action based on the advisor's recommendations.

There are also systems with the ability to link the investment advisor to the participant's account. This method of advice allows the advisor to make changes for the plan participant when appropriate. The advantage of this account is that it is managed and the participant does not have to worry about getting online and figuring out how to exchange funds.

Employers that have not done their homework end up with providers that offer inadequate service and average investments. If you don't understand how a plan works, you won't know whether you have not complied with the govern-

---

[*] The collective works of Edwin J. Elton, Martin J. Gruber (Professors of Finance, New York University) and Christopher R. Blake (Professor of Finance, Fordham University).

ment rules until they audit you or an employee turns you into the Dept. of Labor for fiduciary violations.

Bells and Whistles

The plan document should be written to promote the kind of plan you want to offer to your employees. Who will be eligible and when? When do they get their money out of the plan? Will you allow them to take money while still working? Will you match it and, if so, what is the matching formula? In addition to (or instead of) a match, will you make a company sponsored contribution? (This is often referred to as a "profit sharing" or the "pension component.")

Company Sponsored Pension or Profit Sharing Plan

In addition to a 401(k) plan, successful employers gain a competitive advantage recruiting and retaining employees by providing additional benefits in the form of a defined benefit pension or profit sharing plan. The employer contributes to these plans. Money goes to all eligible employees whether or not they defer any money into the 401(k).

Not generally known is that most 401(k) plan documents have a built-in profit sharing provision. Utilizing the profit sharing plan provision as part of your 401(k) does not create an additional legal plan entity; it is just another account or money source. Therefore, you can have one plan that has multiple purposes. The employer normally determines a profit sharing contribution at the end of their accounting year (known as the "fiscal year end").

All money contributed by the employer is 100% tax deductible, just like any other business expense. Many employers would rather share their profit with their employees than give it to the government in the form of current taxes. Unlike a 401(k), contributions are not determined by each participant: the profit sharing and defined benefit contributions must be spread among the participants using a non-discriminatory benefit formula. Formulas can favor HCE's without being discriminatory. (You can review several formulas in Chapter VII on Plan Design.)

Matching Participant Deferrals

Some employers match employee 401(k) deferrals. Matching is a discretionary contribution by the employer. A match is provided only to those employees who defer some of their pay into the plan. Typically, the match is 25 to 50 percent of what the employee saves. The match is usually limited to a percent of pay.

For example, the most common match is 50 cents on each dollar saved up to 6% of pay. Another way to say it is that if you save 6% of your pay, your employer will give you 50 cents or half of 6%, which is 3% of your pay. Small employers base their match on profitability. Therefore matching is not always offered.

Participant Loans

If the Plan Document allows for loans, plan participants can borrow from their account balance half of their vested amount not to exceed $50,000. This feature is very popular with employees because it makes money available in case of emergency or for long term planning such as a down payment on a home.

The money is repaid through payroll deductions on an amortization schedule similar to a bank loan. The participants pay themselves back with interest (generally prime rate plus 1%). There is a fee to initiate the loan and a fee to maintain the loan. The plan, the employer, or the plan participant can pay participant loan fees. Payments will be amortized over one to five years or fifteen years if used for a down payment on a home.

The downside of a loan occurs when a participant leaves the company. The loan becomes due and payable. If the employee doesn't pay off the loan it becomes income taxable plus a government excise tax of 10% if you are under age 591/2.

The recordkeeper usually an insurance company, mutual fund, etc., are not generally responsible for administration of the loans. They are responsible for the recordkeeping aspects of the loan.

The employer is responsible to ensure that:
a. the participant qualifies for a loan
b. the amount requested does not exceed government limitations
c. the loan is not a prohibited transaction
d. the participant continues to repay the loan while employed
The employer can outsource loan administration through the administrative service provider such as a TPA.

The Annual Meeting

Now that you have a review of all the elements of a 401(k) plan, you need to keep on top of these details. You should get together with your team responsible for the plan and have a meeting every year to discuss the six key elements.

Every year you should invite your plan provider(s) over for a meeting with your staff that assists in managing the plan. Having a meeting is the first part of good fiduciary conduct.

The discussion points below stem from the six key elements of the 401(k) plan. The meeting should be educational and informative by reviewing the following:

1 **Plan Document**: Is your plan document up-to-date with current laws? Were there changes in the law that required a plan amendment? Are you taking advantage of the new rules?

2 **Administration**: Changes in your business should be discussed to see if the plan needs a redesign. Are employees being enrolled in a timely manner? Is your staff working effectively with the provider(s)? Are participant loans and distributions to terminated participants being dealt with in a timely manner? Review procedures to comply with governmental reporting (Annual Return/ Report Form 5500) and compliance requirements.

3 **Recordkeeping**: Are participant statements being sent to participants' homes? Does the record keeper have their correct addresses? Does the record keeper have educational and investment assistance online? Are you and your employees taking advantage of these tools?

4 **Investments**: Discuss the mutual funds track records both measured against peers and benchmarks for the last three and five years. Are the mutual funds in your plan doing better than average (top 50% of all funds in their category)? If not, consider when you should drop poor performing investments. Do the expenses meet benchmarks? Are the overall plan costs appropriate for your size plan?

5 **Education**: Schedule employee meetings for the coming year and review where to put added emphasis. If participation is good, provide information about achieving goals and how to invest. If participation is lacking, discuss ways to stimulate enrollment or consider changing the plan to automatic enrollment.

6 **Fiduciary Responsibility**: If you review all the above, take action when necessary and take notes, you are on your way to fulfilling your responsibility.

(See Appendix II: Plan Fiduciary Checklist" for a comprehensive list of discussion points and action items.)

Summary

1 Employers become a fiduciary when sponsoring a retirement plan and are responsible for all aspects of the plan.
2 Eligible employees sign up to have money deferred from their pay and transferred to investments, usually mutual funds.
3 Employers can add money to the plan by matching participant deferrals.
4 Employee education is a key component to stimulate participation and keep employee interest in the plan.
5 Employers can also sponsor a pension or profit-sharing plan that is paid for entirely by their company
6 Annual meetings with providers are important to meet fiduciary responsibility requirements.

3

Parties to the Plan

A CONFUSING ASPECT OF RETIREMENT PLANS IS UNDERSTANDING WHY THERE ARE SO MANY ADVISORS AND SERVICE PROVIDERS AS PART OF THE 401(K) PLAN. This chapter will define all the roles of the people involved.

Who is responsible for plan investments and for completing government forms? What does a Trustee do? What is the difference between a Plan Administrator and a Third Party Administrator? Who can sell retirement plans? What is an ERISA Attorney?

Those are some of the things you may want to know when sponsoring a 401(k) plan at your company.

When talking about retirement plans, people in the retirement plan profession refer to the employer as the "plan sponsor." Employers not schooled in "pensionese" assume the plan sponsor is the financial institution that sells them the plan. Additionally, all stockbrokers are not registered financial advisors and insurance agents can sell retirement plans that contain mutual funds without being a stockbroker.

It can be confusing, and you should know to whom you are talking and what hats you will wear as a Plan sponsor.

If you are curious about the roles of different parties to the Plan, this chapter will define the people and their roles.

Who are the Players?

Let us first look at the employer that sponsors a plan and put names on all the hats the CEO or owner might wear. The Employer generally becomes the:

Plan Sponsor,

Plan Administrator,

Trustee,

Plan Fiduciary, and

Plan Participant

You will hire one or more of these people or organizations to help manage a retirement plan:

- Financial Advisor
- Investment Company/Mutual Fund
- Insurance Company
- Third Party Administrator (TPA)

There are also government agencies that monitor and license the people you hire to help manage the Plan:

- The Internal Revenue Service (IRS)
- The Department of Labor (DOL), aka (EBSA) Employee Benefit Security Administration
- The Securities Exchange Commission (SEC)
- The State Department of Insurance.

There are different government agencies charged with monitoring and licensing people in the insurance and investment business. The general public tends to group these people together and call them "brokers." There are differences between insurance brokers and investment brokers; however, both can sell 401(k) plans. To make this even more complex, some of the names or titles they use denote specific licensing and fiduciary conduct and others are just names describing who these people are.

The IRS and DOL are the governmental agencies monitoring retirement plans.

Stockbrokers sell stocks, bonds and mutual funds and they fall under the rules set by the SEC. Life insurance brokers sell life, health, disability insurance and annuities. They are monitored by the State Department of Insurance in the state(s) in which they hold a license. Insurance companies can also sell mutual funds through a product they have created known a "variable annuity."

Insurance brokers sell many 401(k) plans because they are already involved with businesses providing life and health and disability insurance. Insurance brokers may be knowledgeable in 401(k) plans but, by virtue of not being a Registered Investment Advisor (RIA), they are not supposed to give advice on investments. Should a licensed stockbroker give advice, they become a fiduciary. Both insurance brokers and investment brokers steer away from giving advice to avoid becoming a fiduciary.

You also need to be concerned that these brokers may be limited in what investments they can sell to you. If their company only offers certain products then that is all you get to see. This is why smart businesses talk to several brokers.

Confused? That's understandable, because (as I pointed out) different agencies have different licensing requirements. (It would be better if licensing requirements were such that everyone in financial services were called Financial Advisors. This would put everyone on the same field of play and take a lot of the confusion out of financial services, but that's not the way it is.)

This brief review of the multiple job functions inherent in the management of retirement plans shows you how complex the situation is. Putting most of these functions under the control of a single provider (such as an insurance company or mutual fund) *does not reduce the number of roles of responsibility — you can have one entity wearing many hats.*

You will need to be even more knowledgeable if you entrust all aspects of a plan to one provider, because, as the plan fiduciary, you are ultimately responsible for plan administration and investments. Ask yourself who is responsible for cross checking the accounting, recordkeeping and reconciling plan assets.

Here is a diagram of the various roles and tasks involved in 401(k) plans. *It does not matter if the plan is bundled under one provider or unbundled as a team approach; these roles and tasks are separate disciplines and are managed independently as separate service departments or outsourced through strategic alliances.*

401(k) Flow-Chart

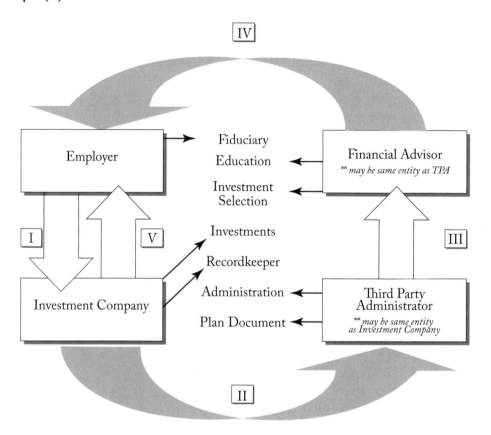

Flow Chart Explanation

I

Employer withholds participant deferral from payroll and forwards money to investment company. Payroll providers with links to investment company can send pay file directly to investment company. Investment company will accept a check or better yet debit employer's bank account via ACH. Investment company is generally the recordkeeper.

II

Investment company is electronically linked to a TPA or their internal administrative support team. Investment company provides data enabling TPA to perform compliance tests, management reports and produce government reports.

III/IV

There is generally a service relationship between the TPA and a Financial Adviser to service the Employer locally. This team provides government compliance, investment assistance, plan design, consulting and participant education for the employer and the plan participants.

V

The investment company as recordkeeper has participant account values and investment information online for the Employer and plan participant. The recordkeeper also prepares participant benefit statements to be sent to plan participants every quarter for self directed plans.

The Plan

The term "Plan" means a "retirement plan," which can be a 401(k) Plan, a Profit Sharing Plan or a Pension Plan. These plans are known as "qualified retirement plans." They refer to employer-sponsored plans that under the Internal Revenue Code Section 401 receive favorable tax treatment.

There are only two types of "qualified" retirement plans: Defined Contribution Plans and Defined Benefit Plans.

Other retirement savings plans for small businesses are called SEPs, and SIMPLEs. These plans are for small businesses and can be less complicated and less expensive than a 401(k). However, they also have less flexibility and generally have lower limits for savings.

Plan Sponsor

The first party to the plan is the employer, also known as the "Plan Sponsor."

The employer is responsible for plan operation and submitting government reports and tax returns.

Any business entity can have a qualified plan. Common entities are sole proprietors, partnerships, LLC's, and corporations. Even a one-person business can have a qualified retirement plan. An employee must work for a business or own a business to take advantage of an employer-sponsored retirement plan.

Individuals can have their own tax-deferred savings plans, such as Individual Retirement Accounts, if the employer they work for does not have a plan. If the employer has a plan, employees may be limited to what they can deduct through an IRA. (Check the limitations online by going to www.irs.gov and search for Publication 590. This government publication gives you all the rules for Individual Retirement Accounts.)

Trustee

The Trustee(s) of the plan hold the legal title to all plan assets. Money that goes into a plan is called a "contribution." The contributions to a qualified plan and the accumulation of plan assets must be held in a trust. A plan's trust is established through a written agreement with the Plan Sponsor. The agreement sets forth the duties of the plan trustee(s). Plan assets in a qualified trust are generally immune from the claims of creditors.

A common misconception on the part of employers is that since employees invest their money through the 401(k) plan, the employees "own" their account. In fact, the *trustee* is the owner and passes through the right for plan participants to invest their money.

Additionally, the Trustee does not have to ask participants permission to change investment providers. The Trustee can change insurance companies or a mutual fund whenever they want. All the Trustee has to do is disclose to the participants what they intend to do at least 30 days in advance of any changes. (Of course, the employer should have a good reason for making the change, such as improving investments or service capabilities.)

A Trustee is usually the business owner who establishes the plan. If the business owner or other company officer does not want the responsibility, they can hire a Trustee. A Trustee for hire is usually an institution called a Trust Company.

Whoever is Trustee has exclusive authority and discretion to manage and control the assets of the plan. When an employer hires a Trustee they can write into the agreement whether the Trustee has complete investment discretion or the Trustee has to take direction from the employer or plan participants.

Most small business owners become the plan trustee because they either do not want an independent Trust Company to be the intermediary or do not want to pay them for this service. Trusteeship for most small-to-medium-size plans ranges from $1000 to $2500 a year.

Who should be Trustee?

Since the Trustee is responsible for the plan assets, do you want to be Trustee and incur that liability? Then again, you are already a fiduciary because you are the business owner, so what is one more hat to wear? However, if you are *not* the business owner, I suggest hiring a Trust Company to limit your liability.

Participant

I have referred to employees and plan participants interchangeably. Technically an employee who makes elective deferrals in a 401(k) plan is considered an "active participant." However, for compliance testing purposes, all eligible employees are considered participants, whether or not they defer any money into the Plan.

Third Party Administrator (TPA) or Professional Plan Administrator

The TPA is a provider of plan services. It is an entity that provides consulting, administration, government reporting and compliance, participant reporting and management reports to the employer. Some TPA's provide investment services and take on the role of Financial Advisor. The TPA is often referred to as the "plan administrator" because it is hired to administer the plan. (The government created a definition for the term "Plan Administrator" but their definition did not consider the role of a TPA.)

Plan Administrator

The Plan Administrator is a person or entity responsible for decision-making involved with the administration of a qualified retirement plan. The Plan

Administrator determines who is eligible for the plan, determines what benefits are due and handles benefit claims and appeals. Plan administrators also have responsibilities to do the following:

1 Distribute documents such as the summary plan description, summary annual report and participant benefit statements.
2 Maintain plan records for at least six years.
3 Provide terminated participants with a written explanation of the rollover and tax withholding options.
4 Determine whether a domestic relations order is qualified.
5 Respond to participant claims for benefits
6 Hire an accountant to audit the plan's financial records (as required by ERISA).

The Third Party Administrator (TPA) is usually not the "Plan Administrator" because they *are not the ultimate decision maker for the plan.* Employers hire TPA's to *assist them* with these duties. See their service contract to determine the extent of their services.

Financial Institution

Financial services companies (whom I refer to as "providers") sell retirement plans. (They can also take on the role of a TPA by doing government reporting and completing compliance tests.) These entities are called insurance companies, broker/dealers (stock brokerages), banks and trust companies. The person who represents an insurance company is licensed as a "life agent," but you know them as insurance brokers. When they represent a broker/dealer, they are called a "Registered Representative," and they too are known as "brokers."

When talking to a broker, ask what licenses they hold. If they are a life agent they can only sell you insurance company products. If they are licensed as a stockbroker they cannot sell insurance company products. They generally sell mutual funds or stocks and bonds.

Insurance Company

An insurance company must be registered in each state in which they intend to sell life insurance and annuities. Annuities can be either guaranteed by the insurance company or contain mutual funds (sometimes referred to by the insurance company as "separate accounts" or "group annuities" or "variable annuities.") Insurance companies can limit their product to only what they manage in-house or make agreements with other investment companies, such as mutual funds, to sell their products.

Financial Advisor

The financial advisor is often referred to as a "broker" or "registered representative." These people are licensed as either a stockbroker or insurance agent and have the necessary license(s) to sell you a investment contract or plan. There are also fee-for-service advisors called Registered Investment Advisors (RIA). Some have all three designations — stockbroker, insurance agent and RIA. RIAs are licensed to give advice and take on a fiduciary status. Stockbrokers generally are not RIAs and are not considered a fiduciary. That means they are not held to the same standard as the RIA. Insurance agents can sell mutual funds packaged by insurance companies under an arrangement called a "variable annuity."

When an insurance agent sells a 401(k) or other retirement plan, it must be with an insurance company. An insurance company's variable annuity is approved by State Insurance Commissioners. The variable annuity is a product that contains mutual funds.

Mutual Fund

A mutual fund is an organization operating under the Investment Act of 1934. A mutual fund manager uses a pool of money to buy a variety of stocks, bonds and other types of investments. Each mutual fund has a stated objective described in the prospectus. A mutual fund is an entity that buys stocks and/or bonds and packages them for you.

You could buy several stocks and create your own portfolio similar to a mutual fund. The issue is then what to buy and when to sell. Therefore, when you buy a mutual fund you are hiring an experienced professional to diversify your money, which helps reduce the risk of large losses. Their job is to buy and sell securities with the goal of making us money.

Internal Revenue Service

To encourage employers to establish and maintain retirement plans for their employees, the federal government provides employers and employees with preferential tax treatment. The Internal Revenue Service (IRS) administers the Internal Revenue Code (IRC), and I am convinced that it is indeed a *code* book — you will need an attorney to decipher its contents. Most of the verbiage in the plan document that you signed indicating you have adopted a retirement plan is taken from the Internal Revenue Code.

Department of Labor

Prior to 1978 there was overlapping responsibility for administration of the provisions of Title I of ERISA and the tax code by the U.S. Department of Labor (DOL) and the Internal Revenue Service (IRS), respectively. Since the reorganization in 1978, the DOL has primary responsibility for reporting, disclosure and fiduciary requirements, and the IRS has primary responsibility for tax deductibility, employee participation, vesting and funding issues. However, the DOL may intervene in any matters that materially affect the rights of participants, regardless of primary responsibility. An agency of the DOL, the Employee Benefits Security Administration (EBSA), is responsible for administering and enforcing the fiduciary, reporting and disclosure provisions of the law. (Prior to 2003 the EBSA was known as the Pension and Welfare Benefits Administration [PWBA].)

What Can Go Wrong?

Problems arise because employers fail to follow the provisions in their plan document.

Here are a few examples:

A An actual situation I encountered involved a business owner who owned more than one company but made no reference in plan documents to excluding those employees from the plan. The plan was audited by the DOL and subsequently disqualified because the employer excluded eligible employees. To reconcile with the government, the employer had to give those employees the same benefits all the other employees received. This was expensive because the DOL made them go back to the time the employees would have become eligible. Additionally, they had to pay substantial penalties and fines.

B Plan documents detail who is eligible and when they can enter the plan. Sometimes employers make agreements with a new executives to have them be part of the 401(k) plan prior to when the document allows. Even though the employer and employee have entered into a legal contract about participation in the employer's retirement plan, that contract (oral or written) does not take precedence over the plan document.

C Plans contain formulas that spell out how to allocate money for matching contributions or profit-sharing contributions. When an employer is not satisfied with the results of these formulas, they consult with their provider about making changes. Often the formulas are adjusted for the calculation, but the plan document never gets amended. However, this means that you are not following the plan document and that can result in plan disqualification.

D Many companies exclude "part-time" employees from receiving full benefits. There is no definition of "part-time" in retirement plan regulations. Employers generally go by group health insurance definition of 30 hours/week to exclude employees from heath benefits, etc. The retirement rule is referred to as "the 1000 hour rule."

According to this rule, all employees who work 1000 hours or more during the "plan year" (a 12-month period specified by the plan document) shall be eligible. Generally, if you exclude employees who work 1000 hours or more (approximately 20 hours per week), you have violated the law.

The employer is the responsible party for all the above examples. I have 90% confidence that when you establish a new plan the administrative service provider will follow the plan document and maintain it for you. However, did they design it according to your situation and is your in-house administrator aware of the plan provisions so that missteps as illustrated above do not occur? Just to make sure you have not broken any laws, have an ERISA attorney review your plan document.

The term "ERISA attorney" refers to lawyers whose main practice is retirement plan law, rules and regulations. There are also TPA's schooled in ERISA. Be sure the TPA or the provider you hired to do plan compliance explains both *your* responsibilities and *their* responsibilities. If they avoid this issue, you should hire an ERISA attorney to review the plan. If you avoid the ERISA lawyer and the TPA, you should consider yourself on your own.

Some providers of retirement plan services are not schooled in ERISA law. Don't work with them! It is a waste of your time and they will get you in trouble. A way to determine whether a provider is schooled in ERISA is to ask about their credentials. Ask about their experience, designations and schooling.

Knowing all the people you can invite to the party provides you with a base of knowledge. You will learn in the next chapter how these partygoers help you start and maintain a plan.

C H A P T E R

The Right Plan

Mystery in Operation

It is common for people to think that a 401(k) plan is nothing more than an investment account at an insurance company or mutual fund with their name on it. However, as you have learned in reading about the six plan elements, there is more to it than that.

Operating or managing a 401(k) plan is somewhat mysterious, for good reason. The mystery arises because the decisions needed to buy a plan from the CEO's perspective are not properly communicated to the employees delegated to operate the plan and the employees delegated to operate the plan do not address their lack of training.

Therefore, the staff member assigned to coordinate the plan for the business is expected to make decisions affecting plan operation without enough knowledge to know if they are doing it correctly. Making decisions without proper education can create significant liability for the business owner and company officers!

Improper plan operation will also drive up the cost of sponsoring a plan. The cost increase will be reflected in excessive time spent by your staff and increased fees by the TPA and auditor. This disconnect is a major reason employers change providers.

Hire an Advisor!

Starting or changing a 401(k) plan can be either a daunting task or made relatively easy with the help of an advisor who specializes in retirement plans for businesses.

You should consider hiring a financial advisor knowledgeable in retirement plan operations (also known as a "Pension Consultant.") They specialize in 401(k) plans as well as all other types of retirement plans. Then they help you find the best plan for your company. They will also develop a policy (known as an "Investment Policy Statement") that addresses how you will review plan investments. Then, if investments are not performing and a change is warranted, the Investment Policy Statement is your road map to make changes.

There are publications that specialize in surveys that tell us who the top 401(k) providers are. However, what is the difference between these providers? Which one is right for your company? What do their services cost relative to the value they bring?

Most companies that want to start a plan or change an existing plan begin with interviewing stock brokerages or insurance companies, because they do the majority of the advertising and marketing. After the investments are chosen, you get whatever administrative services come along with their investment product.

However, you should also interview administrative service firms before choosing the investment company. You can interview administrative service companies (TPAs) from an approved list most insurance/investment companies have.

Most investment providers (such as brokerages, insurance companies, trust companies and mutual fund groups) have similar offerings, so it is difficult for you to know which one will be right for your organization. You need help.

The broker or financial advisor's job is to counsel you on these retirement plan investment providers. Additionally, there is the TPA who manages the overall administrative process, which involves plan documentation, government reporting and compliance and participant disclosure and other plan support functions.

Aligning yourself with a financial advisor and TPA is vital because they become your retirement plan consultants. They will help you manage the process and help you decide which investment company is right for your business. Some TPA firms also act in the capacity of financial advisor.

Bundled vs. Unbundled

Some Employers want one company to handle everything so there is no confusion as to who has responsibility to assist with the plan responsibilities. This is called a "bundled" plan. Others say putting your faith in one company doesn't provide any crosschecks and puts more responsibility on the employer to double check the accounting and compliance issues, so they choose an "unbundled" plan. Unbundled allows you to have a team approach. By engaging a specialized team of experts, they can achieve levels of service and plan designs that are unrealistic for bundled providers. The unbundled approach will also give you local hand holding instead of a long distance call center.

Often you cannot tell if the program is bundled or unbundled because, even though you may assume everything is handled under one roof, the so-called "bundled providers" outsource much of their operations. Bundled and unbundled providers form strategic alliances. Strategic alliances usually create significant cost savings.

> *Often the cost of bundled and unbundled services*
> *can be similar. Therefore don't assume*
> *that because the plan is neatly packaged it costs less.*

Remember that you are a fiduciary. If the amount of money your business pays for services is small but the expenses of the mutual funds are excessive, you may be taking advantage of the employees. The law is very clear that *expenses for retirement plan services must be reasonable.* However, the interpretation of this topic is very subjective. The fees charged for the services you receive will vary depending upon the amount of assets in the plan, number of employees, company locations, depth of management reports and plan design. I suggest you measure the results and value received to determine whether the amount of money expended for the plan is reasonable.

Poor Service

It is not uncommon that the plan provider you chose today will not meet your requirements in the future. But before you "jump ship," call in your current provider to see if their plan or services can be updated. Maybe you just need to revisit your expectations.

It is sort of like buying a house. Just because newer homes have refinements you deem necessary does not mean you cannot remodel. Remodeling could get you just what you need without the expense of moving. Then again, the remodel may still leave you with a backyard that is too small so a move may become necessary.

> *The main reason employers change providers*
> *is because of poor service.*

The Plan Sponsor Picks the Funds

Once you decide who your investment and administrative provider will be, you will need to decide how many and what investments or mutual funds will be offered to the employees. Generally, the investment provider provides all the mutual funds in their offering. Usually this is an overwhelming list. You should get advice on how to offer the appropriate funds for your participants.

You may not know much about picking appropriate mutual funds for your company's 401(k) plan, yet you are responsible for choosing and monitoring the investments in the plan. The financial advisor and his/her team that sold you the 401(k) plan should assist you. All too often, however, the broker or financial advisor depends upon the financial institution to do it for them. So who is taking responsibility for managing the plan investments? 401(k) salespeople do not want to pick funds or give advice for fear they will become a fiduciary.

Regardless of whether you want to put the responsibility on your financial advisor or the investment provider, remember that, as far as the government is concerned, *you* are the fiduciary and are ultimately responsible for the plan's success and operation. So pick an organization that will be a good partner and will take on their fare share of fiduciary responsibility.

> *Tip: Be wary of advisors or organizations that will not help you pick a core group of funds for your employees and help you manage the process.*

It is Employer's job to quiz advisors on why they are presenting the mutual funds in their program. Unfortunately, most CEOs do not ask many questions because they do not know an alpha from a beta (actual investment terms!) and fear they would appear dumb if they asked. Make it your job to learn what to ask!

Perhaps you have heard of a company called ENRON. Their CEO and CFO were fiduciaries and promoted company stock. They could have legally promoted company stock as long as they explained the risks and insisted that participants be prudent and diversify. However, they violated their fiduciary obligations and were charged with fiduciary misconduct. (They were up on many other charges, too, but that is another story.)

You are in the same position when you offer inappropriate investments or keep a poor performing mutual fund in your plan. You are setting your participants — and yourself — up for failure. You do not have to worry too much about going to prison, but the monetary sanctions could be painful.

Investment Company Products

Insurance companies have done a good job of packaging the best funds of mutual fund families. There are many good mutual fund families, and you could go to one fund family to invest all plan assets. You can also find investment providers that offer their competitors' funds. Insurance companies lead the way in this, offering many different mutual funds.

Watch out for those providers who insist you invest in specific funds, generally their own offerings. (A company's own offering is known as a "proprietary fund.") The reason they do this is that they make more money on their own funds. That does not always mean their funds are more expensive, but it may mean their funds may not be the "best in class." Review these funds to see if they are quality offerings.

A few insurance companies do not have proprietary funds and offer many fund choices. This insurance company product is known as a "Group Variable Annuity."

> *An insurance company Group Variable Annuity*
> *is a package of investments ranging from their own proprietary*
> *funds to those of other mutual fund companies.*

The insurance company takes the mutual fund expenses and adds something to compensate themselves for their cost of doing business. They also add something to pay the broker. These costs are negotiable if you have enough money in your plan. In a regular variable annuity, there is a mortality expense because most contracts have some guarantee of principle or the ability to lock in a guaranteed return of income and/or provide a death benefit. Group variable annuities investing in mutual funds do not have any guarantees and the best group annuities are only available to retirement plans. Therefore, their expenses are lower than individual variable annuities. There are also Group Fixed Annuities that guarantee a fixed interest rate just like a certificate of deposit from a bank.

Most group variable annuities have at least 50 mutual funds in their offering. The good thing is that you get a lot of choice, but the bad thing is that too many choices can be confusing. How does the average employee pick funds that are right for him? You should offer enough funds to make the knowledgeable investor happy yet a more limited and manageable group of choices for the uneducated employee.

Support Services

There are two parts to the customer service aspect of your plan. First, customer service representatives help plan participants navigate the web site and answer questions about loans and distributions, and, secondarily, tell you that your question may be of a nature that should be referred to an attorney or the financial advisor.

There is a difference between administrative support and customer service, however. It seems that everyone these days expects good customer service, but having good customer service does not always equate to good administrative support. Here is why.

Administrative support involves compliance technicalities involving government regulations. It is the "how does this 401(k) plan work?" issue. The lower price providers limit these services. If you need help on the technicalities, they will refer you to your attorney, accountant, TPA or broker.

Technical issues about how the 401(k) works can, and usually do, involve advice. As you get into advice, the provider has to be careful not to cross the line of becoming a fiduciary or giving legal advice. Therefore, do not expect much technical help from most 401(k) investment providers.

> *Buying a plan from most 401(k) investment providers and expecting top-notch administration services is like going to a bookkeeping service with your complex accounting issues instead of a CPA.*

Quality Service Costs More

The insurance companies and major mutual fund groups do a lot of advertising, so you tend to purchase their packaged plans. They pay the people who sell these plans (usually referred to as a "broker" or "financial advisor") very little. Generally, brokers are paid only .25% (one quarter of one percent) of the assets in your plan per year. How much in back office and on sight resources can they afford to offer you?

You probably expect them to come out, see you a couple of times a year, and help with employee education. They are also supposed to review and update the mutual funds for your plan because that is why you hired them. Depending on how much money is in your plan, you may not be paying the broker enough to provide quality service and do the required research.

> *Remember the old adage: you get what you pay for. Expect to pay a quality advisor more than .25% of plan assets.*

Open Architecture

There is an alternative to packaged plans called "Open Architecture". This technology allows multiple service providers to communicate and share data electronically.

The financial adviser can offer the plan sponsor more options and control. Open architecture means having the ability to send and receive data from a variety of mutual funds or investment providers instead of being limited to a group of investments in a bundled or proprietary arrangement. In most 401(k) packages you are limited to the investments offered by the insurance company or mutual fund. Open architecture gives you access to an almost unlimited amount of investments.

Providers who offer open architecture have invested in systems that allow ultimate flexibility. They can offer you just about any investment. These arrangements can give you the ultimate in flexibility and usually cost less — sort of like buying a 401(k) plan wholesale.

They All Look the Same

Most 401(k) plans you look at appear similar. You need to be able to judge their quality and value proposition. This is hard to do without a qualified advisor on your team. You will tend to buy the plan from someone you trust. Then, when services fail, primarily because you don't insist that the advisor see you regularly and explain what is going on, you fire him and move to a similar plan that in the long run doesn't produce any better results. (This is sort of like the definition of insanity: doing the same thing repeatedly hoping for a different result.)

> *Rule: Work with an advisor who reviews investments*
> *and helps with employee education.*
> *If they do not initiate annual meetings then you should.*
> *Managing a plan is a partnership.*

Questions to Ask Yourself

First, ask yourself whom the plan will benefit. If you conclude that you will be the one who benefits, see chapter VII on "Plan Design." If the plan is for the employees, recognize that you have a huge responsibility and apply the concepts you learn from this book to make the right choice. There is not any one plan that is the best; however, almost any plan will work if you have an educated and talented staff to manage the process.

Do you want to outsource as much as possible or do expect your staff to do most of the work? Providers put different emphasis on their services. For example, some expect you to manage the loan and distribution process; others do it all for you. Some keep track of years of service for vesting; others expect you to track it. Some providers actually have the nerve to give you a questionnaire that mimics the tax return you hired the provider to complete. Such a questionnaire can take hours to complete, assuming you know where to get the answers.

To avoid having you complete the tax return known as Form 5500, consultants will advise you to be sure the provider gives you a signature-ready Form 5500. What is often overlooked is that the provider provides the form signature-ready after you complete a dozen pages of questions about plan administration and operations. You should not have to answer more than a few questions.

What Do Plans Cost?

Cost becomes a major consideration when it comes to choosing a provider. Larger plans generally have the plan pay all fees, such as investment, administration, record keeping and education costs. Smaller plans (generally less than $10 million in assets) have the plan pay for investment and recordkeeping and education costs and the business pays the administrative compliance, government reporting and auditing fees. This means you need to know all fees being taken from your employees because, over time, fees will affect their retirement income.

According to Morningstar, mutual fund expenses cost, on average, 1.40% of assets per year. Bond funds cost less and international and specialty funds costs more.

As a plan sponsor, you must decide how to divide these costs between your company and the plan. How much should the plan participant absorb and how much should the business pay? The more the participant pays, the more the mutual funds have to earn to make up for the plan expenses.

As a fiduciary, it is your job to be sure plan expenses are reasonable. You do not have to have the lowest cost for your plan to have reasonable expenses, but you must consider the level of service you are receiving or that you require. It is a quality and value proposition. Getting something at the lowest price usually means quality is lacking at some level.

Share Classes

Mutual funds have costs to manage their business. The costs are called "expenses" or the "expense ratio" on their disclosures or information reports. Share classes have different expenses.

Look for share classes that minimize the expense ratio. Share class is noted with a letter such as A, B, C, I, R, etc. "A" shares and some "R" shares have the lowest expenses, but "A" shares have an up-front fee or commission. If you have one million dollars in plan assets, the commission is usually waived. The commission is also waived for amounts less than one million dollars when purchased through most insurance company pre-packaged plans.

Other share classes, such as "B" and "C" shares, do not have an up-front commission but have higher expenses or backend charges. Always ask to see fund expenses and ask if there are any discontinuance or surrender charges.

Most insurance companies have "benefit sensitive" plans which will not assess a surrender charge to plan participants that receive a distribution but may charge the plan a fee if you terminate the contract pre-maturely. There are also investments that are not mutual funds but invest in stocks and bonds just like mutual funds. These arrangements are known as Exchange Traded Funds (ETFs). They can save you money because they have lower internal expenses.

Many retirement plan providers have funds with expenses averaging less than the 1.4% mutual fund average. However, there can be add-on fees for managed accounts, participant education, administration, recordkeeping, distributions, and commissions. Sometimes these additional fees are absorbed by the mutual fund or investment company.

However, just because they bundle additional administrative fees inside the fund expenses does not mean it is free. Businesses providing retirement plan services must make a profit. In determining their fees, they consider not only the amount of money you have in your plan but the average account balance per participant. A plan with 40 participants and two million dollars of assets is more profitable than a plan with 400 employees and two million dollars in assets.

When a provider tells you administration is free or has been reduced in price, they are usually receiving money from the investment company. This means the plan participant may be absorbing some of the cost of operating the plan.

Some people have commented that passing these costs through to the plan participant is ultimately reducing their retirement income. What these people do not consider is that it is more expensive to bring 401(k) plans to the market for small employers. When I have asked employees how they feel about the insurance company adding another one to one-and-a-half percent to the cost of the plan, they all say, "If that means there is someone we can ask for help and who is monitoring the funds for us, then it is worth the money."

Investment Expenses

Plan investment expenses are those fees necessary to operate and manage the mutual fund. Mutual funds call this the expense ratio. Insurance companies refer to their fees as an "asset management fee." These fees are usually expressed as a percentage of assets.

The plan investment expenses can range from more than 3.0% of plan assets per year down to less than 1.0%. The fee is based on type of investments (stocks, bonds, mutual funds, Fixed Accounts, managed portfolios, ETFs, pooled accounts, etc.), plan design, amount of assets and the average account balance per participant. The DOL says fees must be reasonable, considering all relevant factors.

A very small plan (under one million in assets) paying 3.0% for investment expenses is very common. It is not profitable for investment providers to handle small amounts money. Investment providers generally increase their fees for smaller plans. The more assets in your plan, the lower your fees are likely to be.

Studies have been made indicating that a 1.0% increase in investment fees substantially reduces a participant's retirement nest egg. Studies also show that indexed funds beat managed funds more than 95% of the time. Indexed funds cost less so why have managed funds? Your financial advisors job is to find mutual funds or similar investments that beat the index it is associated with. I like to see plans use the top managers who have consistently beaten the indexes, (and have done it net of all fees).

Also managed stock funds can be less risky and give better returns without having to invest in bonds or fixed income investments. I am skeptical of those who say there is no benefit to invest with managed mutual funds because of increased fees. If you have investment managers that consistently beat the indexes you are helping your plan participants in a positive way. If you have no investment advisory assistance then indexed funds maybe right for you.

In any event, it is your job as a good fiduciary to review fees and negotiate reductions as your plan grows.

When Should the Plan Pay All Expenses?

In addition to investment expenses, there are the expenses for government compliance and administration.

Suggestion: Pay plan administrative expenses through the business and let the plan participant pay investment expenses. Administrative fees are fully deductible.

---

*Plan cost comprises investment expenses
and administrative fees.
Investment expenses far outweigh administration costs.*

Example: If plan administrative expenses are $3000 a year and you have $100,000 in plan assets, the cost of compliance and administration is 3%. If the plan has one million dollars, the cost to the plan is .3% (three tenths of a percent). It is not reasonable to have participants pay 3% in administrative fees in addition to the mutual fund expenses.

Summary

Here is a five-part process to help you achieve success when sponsoring a retirement plan.

1 Hire a financial advisor who specializes in retirement plans.
2 Hire a TPA to do government compliance.
3 Establish a plan that allows you to substitute mutual funds that do not beat their respective index or peer group.
4 Design a plan that is appropriate for your business. (Ask you advisors for help)
5 Choose an investment provider that is aligned with a TPA.
6 Offer investment education or hire an RIA to give investment advice.

C H A P T E R

Managing the Plan

IN SMALL COMPANIES, EMPLOYEES GENERALLY WEAR MANY HATS. The person handling benefits may also manage the office, process payroll, pay bills, etc. All too often, there is a general lack of coordination between the business owner and the staff they delegate in-house to manage the 401(k) plan. The lack of coordination can also involve a low cost service provider. Low cost providers take little if any responsibility for the compliance aspects of a plan. This chapter explains what it means to administer a retirement plan.

> *To "administer" means to carry out, control,*
> *direct or manage a process.*

You will be outsourcing the administration of your plan, but there will still be some administrative details for you to handle.

In-house Administrator

Having a 401(k) or other qualified retirement plan is labor intensive and complex. Unfortunately, most people that market these products do not have a good understanding of the amount of work your staff must do to keep you out of trouble. The salespeople presenting their products will assure you that their products contain a responsive account representative, good investments, great materials for employee education, Internet access and that they are priced fairly. What they do not know is how effective your staff will be working with their back office.

The fact is, most employers do not know how effective they will be with a plan provider until after they have purchased the plan. Problems can be avoided by working with advisors who work with many different investment companies. They can counsel you on the best investment provider/record keeper for your business.

The in-house administrator is the contact for the provider you have chosen. Most small businesses have their controller, HR manager, office manager or payroll supervisor handle the 401(k) as the employer's in-house administrator. The in-house administrator needs to know five areas of 401(k) administration:

1 Transferring the money withheld from employee paychecks
2 Helping with employee enrollment (know when employees become eligible and provide accurate enrollment data, i.e.: hire & birth dates and investment choices)
3 Verifying that a participant has terminated employment so they can get their money (distributions)
4 Handling participant loans (Although this function can be completely outsourced, they need to know the rules.)
5 Supplying confidential employee information, as needed, to the TPA or provider. (Supplying inaccurate employee data (which occurs all too often) increases fees).

The in house administrator and senior staff should also be able to answer general questions about the plan.

> *Nothing lowers the perception of a quality 401(k) plan*
> *faster than an employee*
> *that can't get any information about the plan.*

401(k) administrative issues come up frequently. The in-house administrator(s) needs training to understand basic 401(k) administrative routines. They need to learn the terminology so they can communicate effectively. Also, it is quite helpful in fulfilling their position if the individual has some practical understanding of financial principles.

The in-house administrator does not have to be an accountant, bookkeeper or CFO, but if the person does not understand the importance of plan administration things fall through the cracks.

For example, it is the employer's job to transfer the exact amount of money deferred from each employee's paycheck to the investment company/record keeper on a timely basis. The amount of the check or bank transfer has to equal all participant deferrals and loan repayments. If your plan matches employee contributions, the match must be labeled as an employer contribution, not an employee deferral.

It seems simple, but it is not. You also need to monitor the money being credited by the investment company. The investment company will credit the money where you tell them to put it. If your staff does not know the difference between an employee deferral, a loan repayment or a matching contribution, you are in trouble.

When you send information to your administrative provider, it is your responsibility to be sure it is accurate. How would the provider know that you left an employee off the census report? On a similar note, they do not know if you overstate or understate employees' compensation. These errors if caught by the government can disqualify your plan!

> *Generally, employers blame the provider*
> *when there are problems and inconsistencies.*
> *Often it is the fact that an employer's staff lacks education*
> *about the plan provisions and administration*
> *that causes the problem.*

The right 401(k) provider for your business can make your in-house administrator's job a big task or a small part of their overall work load. When 401(k) providers explain their program, they will not emphasize how labor intensive their program is for your staff. If anything, they will try to minimize the work you have to do (if they bring it up at all).

When it comes to establishing a plan for your company or changing the plan provider, it is important to understand to what extent you are outsourcing the 401(k) plan administration functions.

What is "Service"?

As a successful business owner or executive, you want the most for your money so you generally choose a provider who appeals to your pocketbook and who promises good service.

Service has several aspects:
1 service to you as a fiduciary,
2 service to your in-house administrator, and
3 service to your employees.

The criteria used to judge a good provider today will become the general rule to help you maintain your company's retirement plan in the future. Good providers help with:

- services that minimize your fiduciary liability, and
- services to your staff to minimize the time spent working on the plan. (What is the cost to your business if a staff member has to spend too much time administrating a plan you thought you had outsourced?).

Services to the employees' include:

- good investments, internet access, clear and legible statements, timely processing of participant loans, and distributions and investment education.

There is a higher cost associated with good service,
but good service is more than answering your phone calls;
it is keeping you out of trouble.

As a business owner/executive, you should be concerned that you get your money's worth. However, unless you are well schooled in the operation of a sophisticated retirement plan, you really do not have a clue, so you may end up either going with your gut instinct or depending on a handy referral.

> ## *The 401(k) plan is a valuable asset that your employees are relying upon ... Don't take shortcuts!*

Think of your 401(k) providers as employees. Each employee should have a job description and be entitled to meetings with management from time to time to discuss their performance. The roles and responsibilities associated with the plan is the job description.

If performance is not satisfactory, the provider should be told of the issue and given a chance upgrade their service. You do not fire an employee the first time they make a mistake, and your 401(k) provider needs (and deserves) feedback, too.

Automatic Enrollment

Do you want to avoid the enrollment process? If so, design your plan to allow for automatic enrollment. When an employee comes to work for you, inform him or her that you will be taking 3% of their salary each pay period and investing it in the company's 401(k) plan. (You can use any percentage up to 10%, but, practically speaking, you should not exceed 6% because research has determined that many employees will object to more than 6% being deferred from their paycheck.)

Part of automatic enrollment is providing your employees a disclosure notice that says they can decline participation or change the deferral percentage. The notice also says that their money will be invested for them in what is referred to as the default account. This should be a balanced account with approximately 60% stocks and 40% bonds and cash. These default accounts can also have names such as target maturity fund, lifestyle fund or an account managed by a Registered Investment Advisor (RIA). If participants want to self-direct their investments, they must get online and do it themselves.

Employee Deferrals

When employees enroll in the 401(k) plan, they must complete either a paper enrollment form or online form. This form gives the provider information on who they are and where to invest the employee's money. To accomplish this feat, there must be a procedure to get their money into the investment account. (This is called the "payroll deferral transfer" or "deferral upload.")

Each pay period a check for the total deferred by all plan participants is sent to the provider. The money can be mailed or sent by the most popular method, known as "ACH." ACH is the same banking method you use to pay your bills online — you allow the authorized entity to extract the funds from your account.

The employee deferral and transfer of money process is often taken for granted or is totally blown out of portion. More often than not, this process is dependent upon the competency of the person at your office doing the work. Although not a complicated process, it has to be done with total accuracy or the provider cannot invest the money in accordance with the employee's instructions.

Each payroll, the employer or payroll provider is required to get online with the provider and complete a spreadsheet-type program with each employee's name, social security number and deferral amount. In addition to the deferral, you may also be entering a matching contribution and/or repaying a loan made by one or more participants.

Each of these accounts or money sources has a name: employee deferral, employer elective contributions, vested match, safe harbor match, participant loan, rollover, transfer in, etc., are called *"money sources."* When you set up the plan, the provider, and sometimes the payroll vendor, will ask you to identify the money sources on your deferral transfer.

Putting the money into the wrong money source is easier than you might think. You might believe that because all the money belongs to the plan participant these different sources are of no consequence. Mistakes here can be tantamount to putting money in the wrong participant's account. How would you like your money ending up in someone else's account?

What Can Go Wrong?

Here are a couple of things that can go wrong.

Instead of giving credit to the participant for their loan repayment, you lump the money into their deferral account. They are paying down their loan but not getting credit for it. Then, on the other side of the ledger, you are crediting their employee deferral account with more than they authorized you to deduct from their pay.

Another problem can occur when you elect a safe harbor match that must be vested immediately. In some cases, you could have already had a regular match with a vesting schedule. Did you put the matching contribution in the right source? If not, participants may not get all the money they are entitled to.

Do not assume the record keeper will figure out your intentions. The record keeper is processing millions of transactions, so you need to understand sources of money or use a third party administrator (TPA) to help you with these functions.

If your plan has over one hundred eligible participants (an ongoing plan that never had one hundred eligible participants needs to get to 120 eligible participants to trigger an audit), an independent certified accountant will audit your plan. If he or she has to figure out how to reallocate money put into the wrong money source, this can easily double your audit fee.

Who is checking the plan for proper recordkeeping if you have less than one hundred eligible participants?

I was consulting with an employer that did not want to review any reports and assumed that the TPA and investment provider were taking all necessary steps to keep him out of trouble. However, on audit at year-end I found that the payroll department had neglected to deposit two weeks of employee deferrals. The oversight had occurred early in the year but they had never reconciled it, so it went undetected.

Finding the payroll period which was left out and the appropriate amount to deposit was not too hard, but there were considerable time and expenses incurred trying to figure out how much in earnings were lost because the money was not invested for ten months. In addition, employees were terminated and paid out the wrong amounts.

I also discovered that the investment broker that helped set up the plan was no longer in the financial services business and plan investments had never been reviewed. Most of the investments, all six of them, were performing well under their benchmarks and other funds of similar goals.

These issues point to the officers of the company not having had proper procedures and not monitoring their staff. This is referred to as a "lack of fiduciary prudence." The following chapter delves deeply into this topic because failure to be a good fiduciary creates personal liability.

C H A P T E R 6

Fiduciary Responsibility

MOST INVESTMENT ADVISORY FIRMS, STOCK BROKERAGES AND INSURANCE COM-
PANIES WANT TO GIVE YOU GOOD FUND CHOICES, BUT THEY ARE ALSO CON-
CERNED ABOUT MAKING A PROFIT. They understand that many employers find
that "good enough" is their standard. Therefore, I see packaged plans with increased fund expenses with little if any out-of-pocket expenses for the employer.
Some employers only look at what it costs the company and not how the plan
expenses affect their employees. This chapter looks deeply into not only investment responsibility but overall plan administrative responsibilities required by
the government.

Diversification vs. High-Performing Funds

When 401(k) plans were just getting started in the 1980s, many employers stayed away from them because they did not want the liability of investing employee money. This was before participant directed accounts. When participant directed accounts became popular in the early 1990s, employers set up plans at breakneck speed. It was a great benefit with little apparent liability.

Even the Dept. of Labor got into the act to help limit employer liability. It enacted Regulation 404(c), which says, in part, that if you have funds with different risks (such as stocks, bonds and cash), disclose fees, provide education, produce timely benefit statements, etc., you protect yourself from an employee lawsuit if the return on investment isn't what the participant expected.

The stock market soared all through the 1990s, so the issue of mutual fund review and analysis was not given much attention. As long as you offered "large growth" mutual funds, everyone made money. The problem was that 401(k) providers were offering a limited number of fund choices and participants only wanted to put money into the funds that were currently doing the best. Putting money into many large growth funds gives you the illusion of diversification. However, in actuality, most large growth funds invest in the same stocks, so you have not in fact diversified.

When, because they were not properly diversified, participants lost money starting in the spring of 2000, they stopped contributing and others who became eligible didn't want to enroll. Directing your own money in your 401(k) plan all of sudden became very risky. Unfortunately, due to marketing pressure, providers competing for market share promote participant directed accounts.

Enrollment brochures and investment advisors recommend diversification to avoid large losses. The problem is that many novice investors and most of the employers purchasing a 401(k) for their company think all the investments in their 401(k) plan must make money all the time. If you load up your plan with all the best performing funds this year, you are not considering the ups and downs of the stock market. (See the chart called Annual Return for Key Asset Classes in Chapter VIII, Investments. You will see that different asset classes make money at different times.) Having some mutual funds that are out of favor this year doesn't mean they won't make you money next year.

Another related issue is that the packaged plans look very similar, so employers tend to buy the plan with the lowest expenses.

Generally, I must agree that lower cost funds are better, with three exceptions:

1 Measure the fund's return net of expenses. Top-notch mutual managers don't grow on trees. Good managers beat the peers year in and year out.

2 How much volatility is inherent in the fund? An average rate of return of 12% doesn't do you much good when a fund earned 40% in the year before you invested with them and then 5% after you signed up.

3 Understand risk. An aggressive fund may be OK if you are in it for the long run. You have decided you can withstand the volatility. However, most plan participants are risk adverse. Therefore, you should have funds with varying degrees of risk.

As an officer or owner of a business, you are familiar with the complexities of running your business. Sponsoring a retirement plan entails many of the same issues — cash flow, payroll, personnel, sales, administration, and fiduciary responsibility. If you think of your 401(k) plan as a business, it will go a long in keeping you out of trouble with the government and your employees.

Personal Liability

The Employee Retirement Income Security Act (ERISA) contains rules you must follow to keep your company's retirement plan tax qualified. ERISA was enacted to protect the participants' and beneficiaries' rights. You must follow ERISA standards, and the government expects you to know your duties.

> *If you are not willing or able to educate yourself
> and follow through with these responsibilities,
> you must hire someone else to carry out these duties.*

If you are the business owner or trustee, you are personally responsible for your company's retirement plan. Do not be fooled when you hear, "Working with us assures you coverage under Regulation 404(c)," or "We take on the fiduciary liability for you." For the most part, that's just marketing hype.

The marketers want you to believe that you are not responsible for the investment outcome if you hire them and let your participants direct or invest their own money. If you are going to have a participant directed plan, you should be clear on what the rules are to avoid unnecessary liability. For example:

1 When you buy a package of investments, what makes those investments appropriate for your employees?

2 How do you measure one investment company and/or mutual fund against another?

3 What information are you given to judge the investments?

4 If the investments are not performing, when do you change to new ones?

5 Is the information you are given easily understood by lay decision-makers?

6 Have you elected to operate the plan under the 404(c) regulation?

You Can Get Into Trouble!

When it comes to fiduciary liability, just refer to the sanctions levied against officers of Enron, World Com and Xerox. Their actions not only affected their business and retirement plans but also people who invested in their stock. The people investing in Enron, World Com, and others depended on the information they received from the officers of the company to make their decision to invest in their stock. Your employees are similarly depending on you to choose and manage the mutual funds you chose for them.

In 2001, the Dept. of Labor sued First Union, a large company that was offering improper investment choices for their employees. A class action lawsuit was subsequently filed on behalf of the company's 5,000 former employees. The suit dealt with Regulation 404(c). The suit claimed that First Union acted imprudently by failing to investigate whether non-proprietary funds could provide participants with superior-performing and less-expensive options other than its own funds. A second 404(c)-related charge alleged that First Union failed to provide participants with adequate notice of their options when fund changes were made.

The point is that you need to be a good fiduciary or not just the government but your own employees may sue you. In fact, the 404(c) regulation almost makes it too easy for employees to band together to sue you if you do not provide good investments and follow the rules. You can avoid these fiduciary issues and the potential pitfalls of the 404(c) regulation by following the Fiduciary Checklist in the appendix and providing quality investment choices. Employees will have a difficult time suing you if the investments make money and they are getting help in reaching their retirement goals.

Fiduciary Defined

Plan fiduciaries are responsible for the ongoing operation of the plan. The officers, board of directors and business owner are considered fiduciaries.

Sometimes, in an attempt to get the officers of the corporation off the hook, a plan committee is formed with the authority to make investment decisions. The committee becomes the "named fiduciary." However, I have seen the CEOs, CFOs and HR managers actually end up making the decisions. Even though they think they got off the hook by not being named as the "Named Fiduciary," they become a functioning fiduciary and still have liability. In other words, if it looks like a fiduciary duck and walks like a fiduciary duck, it's probably a fiduciary duck!

Plan fiduciaries are expected to act with the "care, skill, prudence and diligence under the circumstances then prevailing that a prudent man acting in a like capacity and familiar with such matters would use in the conduct of an enterprise of a like character and with like aims."* Along with administrative details such as offering the plan to employees when eligible, providing benefit statements, distributing their money when separated from service, providing the government with tax filings, etc., they are responsible for offering plan participants with decent investment choices.**

Even if you feel that your plan is too small for you to worry about the fiduciary standards, you should be concerned about giving your employees a good retirement plan. It is appropriate for your plan advisor to help you analyze the mutual funds in your plan.

The problem is most employers expect this to be done for them just as the investment company automatically sends out benefit statements every quarter. It is *your* responsibility to review the funds in the plan because *you* are the fiduciary. If you are not knowledgeable, then the law says you are supposed to hire some one who is. Therefore, you should work with financial advisors or retirement plan professionals who can help you with this chore.

> *Financial advisors should be able to demonstrate that they have the analytical tools necessary to create and monitor a core group of funds.*

---

* ERISA Sec.404 (a) (1) (B)
** Investment Duties under Dept. of Labor Regulation Section 2550.404a-1

I have previously suggested that the advisor develop a core group of funds and review them regularly. Many investment providers offer eighty or more funds and replace the funds that do not meet their standards, or which are closed by the fund family. All too often financial advisors find employers not willing to pay them to manage the core group and therefore offer all the funds the investment provider offers.

The problem with offering all the funds in enrollment materials is that you are overwhelming most employees with too many choices. Research has shown that the more funds you offer, the less participation you will get. The way to offer many choices without confusing people is by providing Internet access to hundreds of funds but only presenting the core group in the enrollment materials. That way the sophisticated investor can go online, research fund offerings and replace or add to the core group.

You should also expect to pay more to have an advisor manage the core group of funds. The brokerage commission may not pay for this service, depending upon the size of your plan or what fee was negotiated.

Follow ERISA Rules

Employers who do not follow ERISA's guidelines are personally responsible for violations of these rules. You may not even be aware of these violations (known as "fiduciary breaches") until an employee sues you or the government audits your plan and finds the transgression.

Plan participants can sue individually or as a class if they believe you overcharged them or could have provided better investment choices. The problem is that you have to defend yourself whether the lawsuit is justified or just frivolous. The potential cost of defending a lawsuit is high. A 2003 study done by Tillinghast, Towers & Perrin showed that the average defense cost was $365,000 and the average judgment was around $1,000,000!

If you do something wrong that has to do with investments or you create a situation that is determined not to be in the best interest of the plan participants, you can be held *personally* liable. This means your home, and personal assets are at stake. Dept of Labor Interpretive Bulletin 2509.96-1 says a fiduciary is required to make good any losses resulting from a fiduciary breach. (There is a limited exception for self-directed plans that follow DOL Section 404[c]).)

You can avoid unwelcome surprises from plan participants, the DOL and IRS by having an annual meeting with your advisors to review the plans operations.

Delegation of Responsibilities

Delegating the day-to-day liaison responsibility to a staff member is necessary for the practical operation of the plan. Allowing your staff to make policy decisions or establish policy creates liabilities you are unaware of, yet we see this all the time.

For example, payroll information must be forwarded to the investment company to determine how much money is invested on behalf of each employee. The payroll person or payroll company needs to be aware of what compensation is to be used, such as all pay, pay excluding overtime, or pay excluding bonuses, plus what about leave of absence or severance pay?

You may also be sending pay information via fax. This requires hand input by the investment company, which can lead to errors. Generally, the investment company offers internet capabilities. This process is designed to limit errors and speed the investment of employee money.

Think about what defense you would have if employees lost the chance to take part in a stock market rally because you left the decision of how to transmit the money to the person or entity you hired, and they did not do it in a timely manner.

If learning a new process is too much effort for your staff and errors or timeliness of contributions becomes an issue (most often due to your payroll person's inattentiveness) the business owner (you) ends up responsible for not acting in the best interest of the plan participants. As the plan fiduciary, you are required to review all processes involved in the administration of your plan. CEOs generally delegate the review process to their staff, but, in my opinion, the CEO must be involved because of the inherent fiduciary liability associated with retirement plans.

"No way!" you say. "I don't have the time to keep up with all this 401(k) stuff." If that is the case, you should hire an organization that specializes in retirement plans and agrees to be a co-fiduciary to help you with these chores. They will provide timely reports to you and to the government, as well as keeping your plan up-to-date. They will also train your staff and guide them all along the way. Failure to embrace this concept can lead to many plan errors and potential penalties.

I want to give you an idea of some common errors created by employers. This is meant to illustrate the need for some training for your staff. Outsourcing will not solve every potential missed step.

Four Common Mistakes

The following are four common mistakes.

Issue 1: Nondiscrimination Testing

At the end of your plan accounting year, most administrative service providers request that you provide payroll information for the previous year for all eligible participants. (Payroll data is also referred to as "census data" — social security number, name, sex, date of birth, date of hire and compensation.) (Compensation is defined in your plan document. Most plans define compensation as W-2 wages.)

This information is vital in order to perform nondiscrimination tests. Sometimes this information is not requested because some providers use payroll data they received during the year. It is not unusual for employers to ignore the request to update payroll. Most employers do not have a separate database for confidential employee information. Because you have to retype the payroll data off the payroll reports, it is time consuming. For these reasons, the participant payroll data the provider maintains is often incomplete, and incomplete data leads to incorrect test results.

These nondiscrimination tests are known as the ADP and ACP tests. If you do not pass them you are required to return money previously deferred to some HCE's. Failure to get the right information to the administrative provider in a timely and accurate manner can create additional penalties.

The independent auditor for plans with over one hundred eligible participants will find this discrepancy. Smaller plans that are not audited will not know they tested incorrectly until the IRS targets them for audit. There are big penalties to the employer for this transgression. It is also embarrassing to tell valued employees months after their tax year ends that they have to re-file their tax return because the tax deduction was not valid.

Issue 2: Maintaining Terminated Employees

When you have employee turnover, are you unable to find the ex-employees to disburse their money to them? Your human resources department or payroll person makes sure they get their last pay check and COBRA notice, but they rarely have foolproof ways for distributing employees their 401(k) money. Therefore, you are left holding the ex-employees' money until they ask for it. Meanwhile you are paying to keep them on the plan.

One way to solve this issue is a provision in the law called "automatic rollover" which allows you to distribute accounts with less than $5000, but more than $1000. Under $1000, you can just write them a check. This procedure takes care of most situations where ex-employees neglect their 401(k) account. Unfortunately, if they have over $5000, you cannot force them out of your plan. They must request their money. As long as participant money is in your plan, you retain some liability and must continue to provide them with notices and statements.

The government is working on helping you with this issue. They are proposing that if you cannot find ex-employees, you can send their money to a governmental agency. When the employee retires and claims social security, they will be made aware of this money. However, for now you are stuck with employee money over $5000 if the participant does not claim it.

Issue 3: Contribution to a Terminated Employee

When an employee leaves the company, do you manually cut them their final check? If you do that, did you take out their 401(k) deferral and, if you are matching, did you match that contribution? By avoiding the proper processing of payroll, you discriminated against the participant and have potentially disqualified your entire plan over one missed step!

Issue 4: Notification to Employees

When you make changes in the plan document or change investment options, are all participants informed? If not, you are violating several regulations by not informing your plan participants, including those participants no longer on your payroll.

Here is some more insight into issues that can sneak up and bite you.

Can a Fiduciary Breach Happen to You?

If you do not want to or just cannot justify being involved, I do not recommend having a 401(k) plan. You will be at risk as a fiduciary and, from my experience, when the CEO abdicates this responsibility, the plan develops issues or problems.

Does any of this sound familiar? *After* a home is broken into, the homeowner installs a security system. A loved one dies with little or no life insurance. The affected family members make sure they are properly insured so it does not happen to their families. An employee steals from you, so thereafter you trust no one and install more security for constant checks and balances.

Why did these people not know better? They did but never took the time to do something about their responsibility.

> *Take a couple of hours at least once a year*
> *to communicate with your in-house administrator and your*
> *advisors by reviewing the fiduciary checklist.*

For example, if you expect your investment provider to keep your employees up-to-date on which of the funds they offer are performing to their appropriate benchmarks, you may find that they expect the investment advisor that sold you the plan to handle that responsibility. Alternatively, the investment provider may only offer this service if you invest several million dollars with them. A fiduciary breach could be waiting for you. It is not the investment company's responsibility to sell you the best funds. It is *your* responsibility to offer the best funds to your employees!

A Value-Driven, Results-Oriented Process

When involved in this process, try to achieve a value-driven, results-oriented process. Value involves how well the provider meets your needs and how effectively they work with your staff. They should also be flexible, plus have a broad range of investments and plan designs. They should be solution-oriented.

Value is subjective and is usually based on how you perceive sales and service in your own business. Value is not just what one-plan costs compared to another but how well all six elements work together to give you a trouble-free plan.

Results are measured by what kind of job you have done for your employees. Do you have a process that helps your employees achieve their savings goal?

Service providers should offer the following:

1 There should be ongoing assistance with employee education and enrollment.
2 Investments should be analyzed quarterly (annually, for small plans).
3 The majority of investments should be best in class (in the top 25% of all funds in their category).
4 The provider should be expert in ERISA rules and regulations. This means they maintain your plan document and help you with all government compliance.
5 The TPA should have a representative assigned to assist your staff with plan compliance details and participant questions.
6 The TPA should offer training for your in-house administrator.
7 You should not have to approve loans and distributions or keep track of them.
8 You should receive confirmations so you can reconcile all the money sent to the record keeper.
9 Benefit statements and management reports should be provided to you quarterly and be available on the Internet.
10 At year-end, you should receive a Profit and Loss Statement. This enables you to compare the government tax return (Form 5500) with the administrator's valuation and investment company statement of assets.

If they offer these ten points, you are on the way to having successfully outsourced your 401(k) plan.

An investment company should offer many investment choices, provided you have a financial advisor to create a core group of funds for your employees. It's a good idea to establish a core group of around 24 choices and then change fund managers in the core group if they do not measure up. That way, if a fund in the core group shows a trend of poor performance you can drop it and replace it with a similar-style fund that is doing better.

Some investment providers offer this service, but you still must beware. If the provider says they are going to change funds within their offering, what are their criteria? Some providers just do it for you. When the investment provider makes a change without your permission, are their standards appropriate for your plan? They generally make changes for all plans they service.

Making Timely Deposits

The money each employee is deferring must be invested as soon as reasonably possible. This means transferring money coincident with processing company payroll. Failure to do so will cost you the interest and penalties on what the money could have earned. If this is willfully done, the DOL will remove you as Trustee. If you are removed, the DOL will make you hire an independent trustee. Trustees can cost you from $1000 to $5000 a year. To reiterate, you must act in the best interest of the plan and the plan participants.

The law states that you are to send in participant deferrals as soon as possible, but no later than the fifteenth business day of the month following. The DOL has taken trustees to task for not sending off the money as soon as payroll is processed. It seems that if you send in the money within five days, you are okay in the eyes of the government. All investment providers that do the recordkeeping are now handling this process electronically. You should get online to transmit your payroll and either have the money transmitted via ACH or send a check the same day.

Compare your payroll report against the investment company's statement or web site transaction summary. Your HR manager, controller or CFO should be able to get each payroll online and see when the money was invested. Then, each quarter, review the deposits made and match them up with the quarterly report from the provider. The only discrepancy should be one payroll that was processed after the quarter ended.

The business owner (who is also usually the Trustee) is personally responsible for getting the money invested in a timely manner. This is especially important if your investment company is also providing administration services, because the same people that provide recordkeeping of investments do the participant and government reporting and disclosure. You especially need to crosscheck bundled providers. Bundling everything together requires a higher level of diligence on your part.

Pooled vs. Self-directed Accounts

If you match employee contributions or have a Profit Sharing Plan, sometimes you want this money managed for the plan participants. This is called a "pooled" account (as opposed to a "self-directed" account). In a pooled account, you must

invest the money prudently and at "arm's length." That means you do not personally benefit from a plan investment. Even if it is a good deal to buy your building
with profit sharing money, just because it is a good deal for you and good appre-
ciation for the plan, this is not an arm's length transaction. If you want to do this
type of transaction, it is best to go to the government and get their permission
ahead of time.

Plan Money is Not Your Money!

As soon as money goes into a plan, it belongs to the plan participants and beneficiaries, therefore investments must be for their benefit.

ERISA says you must not self-deal, i.e., use money for your own purpose,
even if it results in a benefit to the employees. Rather, the money must be used
for the "exclusive benefit of the plan participants."

If your plan vests employer contributions over several years participants may
forfeit some of the money you gave them, however the money never reverts back
to your company. It belongs to the plan participants either as a reallocation to
participants or to supplement a future contribution.

Who is Responsible for Plan Investments?

You should become familiar with the term "non-fiduciary liability" under Dept.
of Labor regulation 404(c). It is widely assumed (incorrectly, I might add) that
if you offer a full range of mutual fund investments, allow plan participants to
change investments daily, and provide educational materials that you, the business owner, are not liable for lack of earnings due to poor planning on behalf of
the participant. (Please see Chapter X on 404(c) for a complete list of requirements to take advantage of the regulation.)

In addition, it should be noted that 404(c) is not required — it is an option. A
bigger fiduciary problem is not choosing the best funds for your employees and
then not monitoring them. Most small employers do not want to spend the time
with their advisors reviewing investments. Spend the time!

You are responsible for choosing the investments in your 401(k) plan.
ERISA requires that if you do not have the expertise you should hire an expert. Investments should be chosen based on what is best for your work force. If
you know they lack sophistication, they must be given the option to have their

retirement managed for them. You are not off the hook because you allow your employees to self-direct their investments.

The Preamble to the Section 404(c) regulation says:

> *The act of designating investment alternatives is a fiduciary function. All of the fiduciary provisions of ERISA remain applicable to both the initial designation of investment alternatives and investments managers and the ongoing determination that such alternatives remain suitable and prudent investment alternatives for the plan. Therefore, the particular plan fiduciaries responsible for performing these functions must do so in accordance with ERISA.*

Selection and Fund Monitoring

In a participant directed plan it is the employer's duty to select and monitor investment options made available to participants. Furthermore, it may not be prudent to let your employees invest their money without investment advice.

There is nothing in the 404(c) regulation that requires fiduciaries to provide investment advice. However, under ERISA it is clear that if you know your workforce is unsophisticated about investments you have the responsibility to offer them the opportunity to get advice.[*]

The rules under ERISA state that plan fiduciaries discharge their duties *"with the care, skill, prudence and diligence under the circumstances then prevailing that a prudent man acting in a like capacity and familiar with such matters would use in the conduct of an enterprise of a like character and with like aims."*

A prudent man knowing the circumstances would make investment advice available. In doing so, the fiduciary would have a line of defense against a participant claiming that the plan was too confusing and the education incomprehensible. Ask any first-time investor who hears a 401(k) education meeting how much they really understood. Also, ask a participant who has lost money how comfortable he is investing.

A reason some employers give for not offering advice is that they believe that such advice, if faulty, falls back on them. However, the DOL has said that the designation of a person to provide investment advice would not in itself give rise to fiduciary liability for loss or with respect to any breach of ERISA that is the direct and necessary result of a participant's or beneficiary exercise of independent control.

---

[*]   ERISA Sec.404 (a) (1) (B)

It is a common misconception that the employer is liable if they hire an investment manager and that manager has poor performance. Although this is untrue, you still have the responsibility to compare investment managers from time to time and make a change if they are not doing their job.

Know Your Workforce

Before you select the investment provider, sit down with a retirement plan specialist such as a TPA or financial advisor to analyze your company's workforce. Consider your company's size and employee demographics. Consider your employees' knowledge of investments, time to retirement and their ability to get investment advice outside your company.

As mentioned above, the DOL regulation 404(c) is not a requirement and does not get you off the hook as a fiduciary just because you offered the employee's unlimited investment choices. The law is clear that you become responsible if investment choices set up employees to fail. It is not prudent to offer employees all large cap growth funds or funds that have very high risk. Pre-packaged 401(k) plans try to avoid this problem by offering a diverse group of funds. Do these packaged plans give your employees the right stuff?

Investment Policy Statement

Ask your advisor about the need for an "Investment Policy Statement." The IPS establishes the objectives for the management of plan investments and defines the investment process. It lays out how funds are selected, evaluated and monitored.

Most plans do not have an IPS because a detailed IPS requires you and your advisor to take time to review the plan regularly. Most employers expect the monitoring to be done for them at little or no cost. You should expect to pay for this document and ongoing review. The document should be customized to your plan. (Note: The IPS is not a legal requirement.)

The IPS is the road map and spells out the investment review process. It is difficult for a plan participant to make a case against you for not being a good fiduciary if you have a document that details the investment process.

Another alternative is to hire a Registered Investment Advisor (RIA). These people will pick the investments for you and some will even invest the money for your employees. *More employers are going the RIA route because the RIA becomes the investment fiduciary. This means if a plan participant hands their money over to the RIA, the RIA is the fiduciary, not you.* Monitoring an RIA is easier than monitoring each mutual fund's performance.

IPS Annual Review Checklist

1 Review each fund's performance
2 Does the IPS accurately reflect the asset classes and styles of the investments currently being used?
3 Does your policy cover the needs of all participants, considering their level of investment expertise?
4 Are there specific descriptions and benchmarks for each asset class or style?
5 Are their criteria for selecting and retaining fund managers?
6 Is there a process for placing underperforming funds on a watch list? Are there criteria for both removing it from the watch list and removing it from the plan?

Choosing Investments

Most employers pick packaged plans, which means they get investments offered by the provider (an insurance company, trust, or brokerage).

The IPS sets forth the criteria you and your advisor will use to monitor and choose appropriate mutual funds for your company.

For example, if you have funds that had been highly rated but which continue to under-perform their index and their peers, you must discuss why this has happened and whether to replace those fund managers.

What issues arise if you or the investment provider holds onto poor performing funds and the employees lose money for several years? Who is responsible? The answer is: *The Employer is responsible.*

One of the reasons employers move their plans to a new provider is that they are looking for better investment results. The process is easy if you start the process with the IPS, because it will give you the questions to ask the investment provider. The IPS is your investment plan of attack, your fiduciary investment blue print!

The IPS is going to say that you will have investments in various categories, such as large cap, small cap, bonds, etc. Your provider may have a hundred funds and sometimes a self-directed brokerage account. If you want, the IPS could say that the employees can invest outside the core group and that you are not responsible. You then must inform the participants that you review the core group of funds but not the other options.

Court Cases

Here are a few court cases which support my statements about the fiduciary liability of employers involving investments.

Donovan v. Cunningham (5th Circuit Court 1983)

Here the court said, "…the most basic of ERISA's investment fiduciary duties is the duty to conduct an independent investigation into the merits of a particular investment."

Less v. Smith

"[W]here the trustees lack the requisite knowledge, experience and expertise to make the necessary decisions with respect to investments, their fiduciary obligation requires them to hire independent professional advisors." In addition, "fiduciaries have an obligation to select the provider whose service level, quality and fees best match the fund's needs and financial situation." Additionally, "[f]ailure to utilize due care in selecting and monitoring a fund's service providers constitutes a breach of the trustee's fiduciary duty."

Note: The courts in general appear to permit greater reliance on the advice of independent experts whose compensation is not affected by the advice given.

In the *Whitfield case*, the court focused on the advisor and wanted to know whether he had the following credentials:

1 Experience with other ERISA plans
2 Education credentials
3 Registration with appropriate regulatory authorities
4 Reputation
5 References

6 Past performance with investments of the type contemplated

Donovan v. Mazola (9th Circuit Court 1983)
This court decision held that a fiduciary "is not justified in relying wholly upon the advice of others, since it is his duty to exercise his own judgment in light of the information and advice which he receives."

A Lawsuit for Breach of Fiduciary Duty

In the later half of 2006, a St. Louis law firm filed a class action lawsuit against defense contractor Northrop Grumman. A copy of the complaint names the corporation, its savings plan administrative committee, its investment committee, and 16 individuals for "breach of fiduciary duty." The same law firm has filed suits against Bechtel, Caterpillar, Exelon, General Dynamics, International Paper, Lockheed Martin, and United Technologies.

The common thread in all these lawsuits is that the plan sponsor is accused of failing to fulfill its fiduciary duty to make certain the 401(k) plan expenses are reasonable and appropriate.

"The most certain means of increasing the return on employees' 401(k) savings is to reduce the fees and expenses employees pay from their 401(k) accounts. Unlike generalized market fluctuations, employers can control these fees and expenses. Federal law requires them to do so," the suit against Northrop says. The suit also asserts that Northrop Grumman failed to act appropriately to reduce fees for its plan investment options and for the expenses associated with the way Northrop Grumman shares were treated as a plan option.

This is a big deal. According to its most recent SEC filing, the Northrop Grumman plan has more than $11 billion in assets spread over ten investment options plus company stock. Northrop matches 100% of the first 2 percent of employee contributions, 50% of the next 2 percent and 25% of the next 2 percent. Altogether, the employer match totals 3.5% of participating employee's payroll.

Employees can choose between a US equity fund, a US fixed-income fund, a stable value fund, a balanced fund, an international equity fund, a small-cap fund, an equity index fund, a high-yield bond fund, an international bond fund, an emerging markets fund, and a "Northrop Grumman fund" for company stock. Employees can also choose a Schwab brokerage window account.

Northrop Grumman discloses all this on their form 11-K but nothing about the expenses of the plan options.

The most interesting part of the suit is the accusation that the Northrop Grumman plan is filled with "shadow index funds" that are charging fees similar to actively managed funds. It is stated in the suit that Northrop plan participants are paying for active management but not getting it. Therefore, the company and its executives presumably have breached their fiduciary duty.

Shadow index funds (also known as "closet index funds") pick funds, so they are not a real index. However, in practice, their returns will not fall far from their benchmark.

To decide whether a fund is a "a shadow index fund," we look to a statistic called the "R-squared," which measures how much of a fund's performance can be explained by an index. When the R-squared is 95 or higher, signifying that 95 percent of its performance can be attributed to an index, a fund is considered a shadow index fund.

Among well-known retail funds, Fidelity Trend Fund and Dreyfus Fund both have R-squares of 98 percent. While it is possible to manage an index fund for expenses as low as 10 basis points, according to Morningstar, Fidelity Trend has expenses of 83 basis points (.83%) and Dreyfus has expenses of 71 basis points (.71%).

According to the lawsuit, every single one of the nine fund offerings that claim active management have scored as shadow index funds over the last six years. Consequently, corporate management may have been paying two or three times as much as their fiduciary duty would dictate.

Therein lays the problem. Were they overpaying for funds they could have purchased elsewhere for considerably less money? This will be hard to prove because the lawyers suing have no way of knowing what results, quality and value proposition the employer is receiving.

Conclusion

Is your in-house administrator effectively dealing with these issues? Maybe they are aware of these details, maybe not. They are also busy with many other tasks and may not be trained to look for these issues. A good TPA will train and help you manage this process. This is part of the value proposition a good service provider offers.

When I tell CEOs of these issues at the startup of a new 401(k), they do not put a high value on these or most administrative issues. They assume everyone involved understands what can go wrong and has procedures to avoid problems. Unfortunately, this is not the case with many providers. These "minor" issues might appear to be inconsequential but can cost you severe penalties and embarrassment!

Do you review your Financial Statement when presented to you by your accountants? Do you review your company's budget and approve major purchases? Do you review sales quotas and hold executive meetings about trends in your marketplace?

If you do, add another four hours a year to your duties and hold a meeting once a quarter to review the items found in the fiduciary checklist. It will help your staff be more efficient and you will get the kind of plan that your employees will enjoy. As an added bonus, you will stay out of trouble with your employees and the government.

Summary

- Team up with an advisor that will help manage the process of reviewing the funds.
- Consider a Registered Investment Advisor (RIA), lifestyle or target maturity to help your employees invest their money.
- Send in your employee deferrals each payroll and audit the receipt of the money.
- Maintain an Investment Policy Statement (IPS) and follow it.
- Pick your provider based on their ability to help you with your fiduciary duties.

C H A P T E R

Plan Design

MOST 401(K) PLANS SHOULD BENEFIT EVERYONE WORKING AT YOUR COM-PANY. However, plans can be designed to provide benefits to select groups of people who, when tested based on government rules, are determined to be non-discriminatory.

In this chapter, I will introduce you to some basic concepts of 401(k) first and get you acquainted with how some of the non-discrimination rules work. I will then explain how to build additional plans on top of the 401(k) to get more benefits to the business owner and executives while providing significant benefits for all employees at little if any cost to the employer.

Designing an Effective Plan

The purpose of tax-deferred savings is to encourage employees to save for their retirement. Retirement plan tax advantages are structured to strike a balance between providing incentives for employers to start and maintain retirement plans and ensuring that employees receive a fair share of the benefits.

Plan design determines who gets the money or benefits and how much. It is almost common knowledge among employers that there are limitations on how much you can save in a plan. What is not commonly known is that through plan design and attention to your company demographics you can usually obtain results that are more favorable.

Example

I was asked by a financial advisor to meet with his client to discuss why they did not have a 401(k) plan. They insisted they could not have a 401(k) plan because their employees did not want to participate in the plan. Most of his employees were factory workers earning less than $10.00 an hour and required every penny to make ends meet.

A plan was designed to be offered to everyone but mostly office staff signed up. This plan design is called "safe harbor matching." The employer only matches those employees that defer money into the plan.

HCE and NHCE

The government has classified employees into two categories, Highly Compensated Employee (HCE) and Non-Highly Compensated Employees (NHCE). Somehow, in our Congress' infinite wisdom, they determine what amount of earnings classifies an employee as highly compensated (currently $100,000).

Check with your advisor or provider on the amount of compensation that puts you in the highly compensated category, because the dollar amount changes from time to time. There is also a salary cap of $225,000 that is adjusted in $5000 increments based on cost of living. Generally, if you are being paid the maximum dollar amount allowed by law you will receive the highest benefit for the lowest overall cost.

As a HCE, if you want the maximum tax deferred savings in a 401(k) plan you must have a sufficient number of employees in the NHCE category participating. There is a non-discrimination test done annually that measures the average percentage of savings by all eligible NHCE and compares it to the average of what is being saved by the HCE's. In many small businesses the employees are not saving enough for the owner and other HCE's to save up to the government maximum. In order to save the maximum you need the proper plan design.

HCE Limitation

While most HCE's want to save up to the maximum dollar amount, NHCE's in small company plans save an average of 3% to 4% of their pay. If the average savings of the NHCE workforce is 3%, then the HCE's can defer 2% more *on average* or 5% of salary *on average*.

What is meant by "on average" is based on an interesting calculation: It is not the dollar value saved but the *percentage* of your compensation. If the average savings of the NHCE's is 3% and there are three HCE's, they are all limited to 5% of salary as their deferral limit for the year. How can the HCE's save more if the NHCE's do not save enough?

If you are a HCE making $150,000, saving 5% is $7,500, not anywhere near the $15,500 limitation. If one HCE defers nothing the average for the other two goes up to 7.5%; if two do not defer, the maximum for the one remaining is 15%. Limiting other HCE's is one method that will help pass the ADP/ACP (Actual Deferral Percentage and Actual Contribution Percentage) Test. The ADP test is for all eligible participants and the ACP is for employer matching contributions.

Safe Harbor 401(k) Plans Defined

When electing a safe harbor plan, HCE's can defer the maximum allowable.

A safe harbor 401(k) plan is a 401(k) plan under which an employer will no longer be required to perform nondiscrimination testing of elective contributions or matching contributions. To qualify for safe harbor, a 401(k) plan must meet certain employer contribution requirements:

1 A dollar-for-dollar match on elective deferral contributions up to 3 percent of compensation and a 50-cents-on-the-dollar match on elective contributions between 3 percent and 5 percent of compensation, or 2. 3 percent of compensation non-elective employer contributions. (This must go to all eligible employees, whether or not they defer pay into the plan.)

> *Creating a safe harbor plan is the best way to allow the HCE's to save up to the maximum dollar limit.*

Employer Elective Contribution

The employer can make discretionary contributions to all eligible employees whether or not they participate in the 401(k) plan. Most 401(k) plans already have a provision for this additional contribution. If not, you can add the provision to your 401(k) plan by amendment. You do not have to add a second plan to make this additional employer contribution. (We call this an "employer elective contribution" or a "profit sharing plan.")

A profit sharing plan allows the business owner and other selected employees to save up to the government maximum of $45,000 (as of 2007). From time to time, the government can increase this limit, called a "cost of living adjustment." With the maximum 401(k) deferral limited to $15,500 with a $5000 catch-up for employees age 50 or over, a profit sharing plan can add an additional $29,500 to $34,500 of tax deferred savings to the key employees. The employer taking advantage of a profit sharing contribution must also include eligible employees. The additional expense can be as low as 3% or as high as 10% of the salaries of the employees participating in the plan.

The reason many employers do not have profit sharing as part of their 401(k) is because in order to get the HCE's the maximum of $45,000 the employer has to give something to all eligible NHCE's, and that can be expensive. This is why it is important to have the proper plan design.

Leverage

The concept of leverage or *tax advantages* works as follows. You are a business owner and you are paying 40% in Federal and State taxes, you are left with 60 cents on each dollar after taxes. For example, if you made $150,000 in salary, the next $100,000 you want to take home is actually worth only $60,000. The government got $40,000! Each additional dollar you want to take home really equates to only 60 cents in added income.

What would you rather do: A. Give the government the $40,000 or B. Give the money to your employees?

Example: If you are looking at paying $40,000 in taxes on $100,000 that the business is about to pay you, a plan can be designed where get you 75% or $75,000 and your employees get $25,000. This is tax leverage. It also creates a great benefit for the rest of your employees.

Again, if you take home an additional $100,000 you are left with $60,000. Ask yourself if you would rather have $75,000 working for you in a tax deferred in a retirement plan rather than taking home $60,000 which, if you do not invest, you will probably spend.

Inside a retirement plan, you can buy and sell mutual funds or stocks and bonds without paying taxes on the interest, dividends or capital gains along the way. You pay ordinary income tax on all the money only as you withdraw it, when hopefully you are in a lower tax bracket.

Add Additional Plans

Now that you have the concept of tax leverage, let's take the 401(k) deferral and add the profit sharing part and create still another plan called "defined benefit" to get even more money into the plan for the HCE's.

Employers often want to maximize the benefits for their senior executives, owners and their family members. However, they still want to control the cost to non-owner employees. Thus, the dilemma that most employers face is whether to have a plan that may cost them a lot of money for their staff. The only way to decide is have your plan consultant design a few plans and see how the numbers come out.

To give you a better understanding of the various plans available, let us review how profit sharing and defined benefit plans work and define some terms.

Two Types of Retirement Plans

There are only two types of qualified retirement plans: Defined Contribution and Defined Benefit.

Defined Contribution Plan: A Defined Contribution plan is a type of retirement plan in which the amount of the employer's annual contribution is specified. Employers can contribute and receive a tax deduction for up to 25% of eligible plan participants' compensation into a Defined Contribution plan.

Most plans base their contributions on the payroll (gross W-2 wages) of the employees eligible for the plan. Each participant has an account and gets a percentage of their pay contributed to their account. Earnings are allocated back to each participant based on the percentage of their money compared to the total in a pooled plan. This is referred to as a "prorated allocation."

For example: your pay can be represented as a percent of all pay at your company. As an owner, if your pay is 50% of the payroll, you would receive 50% of the money contributed to the plan, as well as 50% of any earnings or losses. The money is then invested by the plan on behalf of all plan participants. This is called a "pooled investment plan."

Alternatively, the employer can allow each employee to invest his or her own money. This is known as a "self-directed plan." In a self-directed plan, each employee invests their own money and takes the gains or loses irrespective of what happens to everyone else.

These Defined Contribution Plans are referred to as either 401(k), Profit Sharing, Money Purchase Pension, or Employee Stock Ownership Plans. Since benefits are based on the accumulation of deposits throughout the years, Defined Contribution plans favor younger employees because of the length of time they have to receive contributions.

Defined Benefit Plan (DB): A defined benefit (DB) plan is a type of retirement plan that specifies how much in benefits it will pay out to a retiree at retirement age. The DB Plan tends to favor an older population because of their shorter time span to contribute. This results in higher tax deductible contributions than with other types of plans.

A plan can say that if you retire at age 65 you will receive 100% of your salary for life. Once the benefits are determined, the employer must contribute a prescribed amount each year to accumulate enough money to reach a lifetime pension of 100% of salary. Generally, contributions can be as high as $250,000 a year. Changes can be made to increase or decrease this commitment, but changing the contribution is not easy. You should think of the required contribution as rent, because once you commit to a contribution you should count on making the same contribution every year.

A word of caution! Sometimes businesses get a windfall profit and establish a DB for one year to shelter the money from taxes. The government frowns on companies that set up these plans with the intention of stopping them the next year. They view this situation as potential tax fraud.

I do not recommend a DB plan if you are thinking of maintaining it for less than five years. However, you can always stop a plan or reduce the contribution if you have a good business reason. (See Chapter XVII on "Defined Benefit" to understand how this type of plan works.)

Maximum Leverage

According to current rules, the amount of contribution that may be deducted by the employer for each year is limited to the greater of the DB plan contribution or 25% of all eligible compensation. This limit applies to employers maintaining more than one plan with at least one common participant in each plan. If the plans are designed not to have the same people in each plan then the defined benefit limitation can exceed 25% of compensation. In fact, there is no percentage limit.

Combine Plans

If you combine the two types of plans and divide up who is in each type of plan, the owners can increase their savings from the defined contribution limit (currently $45,000 and $49,000 if 50 years old or over) to over $250,000 per person under the Defined Benefit Plan. Here is what must be done to accomplish this:

1 Establish a DB plan for the owners or the selected group of employees.
2 Establish a Defined Contribution plan (likely a Profit Sharing plan) for the remainder of the employees.
3 Establish a 401(k) plan for all employees where all employees are allowed to defer part of their salary. No employer contribution will be made to this 401(k) plan.

The chart following shows a combination of Defined Benefit and Profit Sharing plans. The cost to the employer called the "plan annual deposit". As you can see, not all employees are in the same plan. If all employees were in the defined benefit plan, the deposit or cost would be substantially higher. Having more than one plan is a design technique to provide substantial benefits to owners and cover employees that would have gone without a plan if it wasn't for this plan design.

Plan Combinations

		PENMAX Plan Combination	
		Defined Benefit	**Profit Sharing**
		Plan Annual Deposit	Plan Annual Deposit
Participants			
Owner	$ 205,000	$ 250,000	
Owner	$ 205,000	$ 220,000	
Employee 1	$ 59,000	$ 12,980	
Employee 2	$ 33,500	$ 7,330	
Employee 3	$ 105,000	0	$ 13,650
Employee 4	$ 68,000	0	$ 8,840
Employee 5	$ 51,500	0	$ 6,695
Employee 6	$ 33,000	0	$ 4,290
TOTALS	$ 760,000	$ 490,310	$ 33,475
TOTALS FOR OWNERS	$ 470,000	Owners get 90% of the money	
ALL OTHERS	$ 53,785		
TOTAL	$ 523,785		

Note: The illustration above is at the high end of the scale. Most owners put in less money but the leverage is still 90%!

How it All Works

Since the DB plan will favor the older population, more contributions will be allocated to the defined benefit plan, while the profit sharing plan participants would receive at least a minimum contribution of 7.5% of their pay (this is a contribution generally accepted by the government). In addition, with the existence of a 401(k) plan, all eligible 401(k) plan participants are allowed to supplement their retirement benefits with their own deferrals.

Since the DB and the profit sharing plans do not cover the same employees, the employer can deduct contributions made to each plan without being subject to the deductibility limit of 25% of payroll (as discussed above).

One more rule: All DB plans must satisfy a minimum participation test that calls for each DB plan to benefit at least the lesser of 50 employees or 40% of all employees of the employer.

Many have asked how it is possible to have different types of allocations/benefits within a plan that would favor the selected group of employees when qualified plans cannot discriminate in favor of highly compensated employees (HCEs). It is allowable because the IRS regulations allow us to test for discrimination based either on the contributions that the employer makes or on the retirement benefits these contributions can provide.

For most small businesses, testing the benefit at retirement rather than the contributions produces a more favorable result for key executives. This is because the amount of benefit that can be provided by any contribution level depends on the participant's age.

The defined benefit part of the plan will be primarily for HCE's, producing a higher tax deferred current contribution. The profit sharing plan will cover everyone else. Measured to everyone's projected retirement age, everyone gets approximately the same benefit. The government deems this not to be discriminatory. This is one way you explain the different plans to your employees. Everyone gets the same benefit at retirement. The chart above shows the plan contribution made by the employer.

This plan design is one among several available, and each design depends upon the demographics of the plan's employee population as to how well it will leverage.

The method of testing whether this allowable is referred to as "cross-testing" and is based on regulations under Section 401(a) (4) of the Internal Revenue Code. These regulations set forth the rules for determining whether a retirement plan discriminates in favor of highly compensated employees. Though these rules are considered very complex and restrictive, they contain objective tests to determine whether a plan discriminates.

More Plan Designs

This "combination of plans" design is for profitable companies with large salary disparities between employees and owners. It is based upon the employees ages, years of service, and compensation of your company's owners and employees.

You choose employees for each group; each group or tier can offer different benefits, such as:

Group A: consisting owners and family members,

Group B: consisting of managers,

Group C: all remaining employees.

Here is illustration of a company with an employer group with two owners and five employees. Let's look at the leverage.

This is a design with an owner and spouse. The spouse works 1000 hours per year. We divided the spouse's wage between salary and deferral. Your contribution will vary depending upon your budget and the ages of your HCE's.

401(k) Safe Harbor I Cross-Tested Plan

Name	Income	Employee Deferral $	EE %	Safe Harbor Contribution	%	Catch up $	%	PS $	PS %	Total $
Owner, H	210,000.00	15,000.00	7%	6,300.00	3%	5,000.00	2.38%	21,700.00	10%	48,000.00
Owner, W	18,000.00	15,000.00	83%	540.00	3%	0.00	0%	1,650.00	9%	15,100.00
Highly Comp Total	$ 228,000.00	$ 30,000.00		$ 6,840.00		$ 5,000.00		$23,350.00		$ 63,100.00
Employee, A	50,000.00	0.00	0%	1,500.00	3%	0.00	0%	1,000.00	2%	2,500.00
Employee, B	30,000.00	0.00	0%	900.00	3%	0.00	0%	600.00	2%	1,500.00
Employee, C	27,000.00	0.00	0%	810.00	3%	0.00	0%	540.00	2%	1,350.00
Employee, D	40,000.00	0.00	0%	1,200.00	3%	0.00	0%	800.00	2%	2,000.00
Employee, E	39,000.00	0.00	0%	1,170.00	3%	0.00	0%	780.00	2%	1,950.00
Non-Highly Comp Total	$ 186,000.00	0.00		$ 5,580.00		0.00		$ 3,720.00		$ 9,300.00
GRAND TOTAL	$ 414,000.00	$ 30,000.00		$ 12,420.00		$ 5,000.00		$27,070.00		$ 72,400.00

Notes:
The owners receive 87% of the money.
If the owners did not have a plan either the corporation would pay taxes on $72,400 or the owners would bonus themselves the money.
Either way the tax would be approximately $26,000. The contribution to the employees is 5% of their pay, which in this example is less than what the employer would have paid in taxes. This plan design benefits both the employer and the employees.

Other Plans to Consider

There are several other types of plans to consider before implementing a retirement program for your business.

Retirement Plan Comparison		
Topic	**Pros**	**Cons**
Defined Benefit Plan	• Favors highly paid employees • Higher contribution limits • Higher company deductions • Coordinates with other plans • Vested contributions	• Mandatory contributions • Higher administration fees • Less flexibility • Increased fiduciary liability
Traditional 410 (k) Plan	• No mandatory contributions • More flexibility • Less fiduciary liability • Self directed accounts • Profit Sharing Plan is permitted • Loans are permitted • Vested contributions	• Non-discrimination testing • Monitor investments • Increases HR functions • More administrative details • Transfer deferrals regularly
Safe Harbour 401 (k) Plan	• No non-discrimination testing • Higher company deductions • Maximize HCE contributions • Profit Sharing is permitted • Loans are permitted	• Mandatory company 3% contribution or 4% Match • Company contributions 100% vested immediately • Annual commitment • Must notify employees every year about Safe Harbor
New Comparability Profit Sharing	• Discretionary contribution • Can discriminate between classes of employees • Flexible %s between groups • Can reward key people • Can integrate Profit Sharing with year end bonus program	• More testing to stay in compliance • 5% contribution to participants if owner receives 90% of the assets • Higher administrative fees

C H A P T E R

Investments

ONE DAY THE NOTED AMERICAN HUMORIST WILL ROGERS WAS ENGAGED IN A CONVERSATION ABOUT INVESTING. He said one should study the markets carefully before buying a stock, then ... "When the stock doubles, sell it." "But what if the stock doesn't double?" Rogers was asked. He replied, "If it doesn't double, don't buy it."

Investing for Retirement

It would be nice to double our money, but retirement plans offering self-direction stick to mutual funds that tend to be more conservative. Nonetheless, the "Rule of 72" says that you will double your money in a certain amount of time if you know what you will earn.

Here is how the rule of 72 works:

You first write down how much you expect to earn, assume 8% per year. Divide 8 into 72 and you get nine years. It will take nine years to double your money if you earn 8% per year. At 10% your money will double every 7.2 years.

Moreover, at 3 % money doubles every 24 years.

You can see how important it is to try and make a higher return on your investment. (Keep in mind that this equation assumes a constant percentage return and that is difficult to obtain, but you get the idea.)

To understand investments you need to understand types of investments, styles of investments and categories or assets classes.

> *Remember:*
> *the more knowledge you have about investments,*
> *the better position you are in to make good decisions.*

Investment Types: Cash, Bonds and Stocks

There are three investment types generally found in 401(k) plans:

Cash investments have a steady rate of return and little if any risk. Cash investments include savings accounts, money market funds and fixed accounts offered by insurance companies. There are also accounts called "Stable Value" accounts that, although not guaranteed like fixed accounts, rarely lose any money. These investments are a good way to have quick access to your money and protect your original investment from any decrease in value. Although cash investments are a good way to help protect your money, it doesn't have as much income-producing potential as bonds.

Bonds are contracts or IOU's issued by corporations or the government that pay you interest on your money. Bonds are loans. When you buy a bond, you are loaning money to the bond issuer. Essentially, when you buy a bond you are lending money to an institution that, in turn, pays you back a set amount of interest.

Bonds offer more growth potential than cash and are considered conservative investments with little potential for growth other than the interest paid. The potential for growth with bonds may occur when interest rates decrease. At that time, someone may be willing to pay more than the face amount of the bond and that increases the bonds' return upon sale.

Stocks have greater potential for growth. A stock is a share of ownership in a company. When you buy a stock, you actually own a small piece of a company. Buying stock is like buying a house, and owning stocks can have the same result as owning a house. You pay the going price for the property and trust that when you are ready to sell you will get more than what you paid, but sometimes the house does not gain in value because conditions in the area or in the economy cause the house not to sell for what you paid for it. (You should know that most plans today offer real estate as an investment option.)

Investment Styles

Each investment style — cash, bonds and stocks — has an objective or purpose. Let's look at each purpose and their advantages and disadvantages.

Investment Type	Cash	Bonds	Stocks
Purpose	Readily Available	Pays Income	Grows in Value
Advantage	Steady Value	Produces Income	Helps Protect Against Inflation
Disadvantage	No Inflation Protection	Minimal Growth	Value Fluctuates

As you can see, each investment type has a purpose, and for a given purpose, there is an advantage and disadvantage. Professional investment managers decide how to use the various investment types to make money. When professional investment managers buy many stocks and bonds and properly register their company with the Securities and Exchange Commission (SEC) they create what is known as a "mutual fund." Instead of researching what stocks and bonds to buy, we invest in a company called a mutual fund. They sell us shares in their portfolio of stock and bond investments. If they do a good job buying stocks and bonds, the share value increases and we realize a profit when we sell the mutual fund.

In company-sponsored 401(k) plans, you generally do not have the option to invest in individual stocks and bonds. Instead, stock and bond fund mutual funds are used. These funds are made up of many stocks or bonds and are professionally managed. In a bond fund, bonds are bought and sold, or reach maturity.

Because bond funds are being bought and sold, the bond fund never reaches a maturity date. Therefore, the value of a bond fund can fluctuate. (The value of bond funds tends to move in the opposite direction of interest rates. When interest rates go up, bonds tend to go down in value.)

There are many kinds of bond funds:
- Short term
- Intermediate term
- Long term
- Government
- International
- High yield bonds (unrated bonds)
- International bonds
- Blends of any of the above

Just as plans use bond funds instead of individual bonds, plans use stock funds instead of offering individual stocks. These stock funds are made up of many stocks. The managers buy and sell stocks for the benefit of the people who bought shares in their fund. Just as there are many kinds of bond funds, there are many stock funds. Each of these funds invests in different kinds of companies. We call this their "asset class." Just as there are bonds issued by corporations and the state and federal government, stocks invest in different categories.

Asset Classes

There are four main stock categories or asset classes: large-cap funds, mid-cap funds, small-cap funds, and international funds. ("Cap" is the abbreviation for capitalization; "capitalization" is what a company is worth.)

When Bill Gates created Microsoft as a public company and started to sell stock, it was a **small-cap** company.

Do you think there is more or less risk investing in a start-up company? Right — more risk. More often than not, small companies do not make it. However, when they *do* succeed, those who invested in them can make a lot of money.

When a small company grows, they become **mid-cap**, and if they continue to grow, they become **large-cap** companies (such as General Motors, Ford, Motorola, Intel and Microsoft).

These asset classes usually do not all make money all the time. In fact, in some years they may lose money. To give yourself the likelihood of making money every year you should spread your money around between the asset classes. Some money in large cap, some in mid or small, and some in international is a recommended allocation.

Stock-Buying Philosophies

Within each asset class, the manager adopts a style. This style is the manager's stock-buying philosophy. There are three styles: Value, Growth and Blend.

Think of investing for **value** like buying a regular TV. It is affordable and works well but does not have all the bells and whistles such as on the newer flat panel sets. They have been around for a while and they are dependable. Think of Sears and Wal-Mart.

Then there are rear projection TV's. They use LCD technology and are a "**blend**" of regular TVs and the classier flat panel variety. Blend funds invest in both value companies and growth companies.

Then there are the flat panel LCD, plasma and DLP technology sets. These would be in the "**growth**" category, investing in high performance stocks. Think of Microsoft, Motorola and Pfizer.

When looking at investment style, the terms "value," "blend" and "growth" work in a similar fashion. "**Value**" stocks might be the stock of companies that have been in business a long time. Their stock price may be low due to the economy and factors affecting their industry. "**Blend**" stocks have value and growth characteristics, while "**growth**" stocks push for higher returns (but at a higher risk).

As you have learned, assets classes have various styles (such as small, medium and large cap stocks) and invest in value companies or growth companies. If they invest in both they are a blend.

A mutual fund ratings company called Morningstar** developed the following chart to illustrate the various styles. It has come to be called the "Morningstar Style Box."

---

* *Morningstar is the trademark for the Morningstar, a global investment research company.

	Value	Blend	Growth
Large companies			
Mid-size companies			
Small companies			

Ask your investment advisor to fill in the fund names of the funds in your 401(k) plan in the style box so you can easily see whether your plan has the needed diversification. However, it is not necessary to have funds in every style to be diversified.

Recap

1 Know where to get information about the purpose of each fund in your plan.
2 Understand that there are advantages and disadvantages to each of the various investment styles.
3 Be sure to have a mix of cash, bonds and stocks as investment alternativ es and review the mix every year.

Asset Allocation

This next lesson involves how to choose funds in various asset classes.

There are three things you need to learn when diversifying or allocating money. Think of it as if you were going to take a vacation. If you are going on vacation, you need to determine the *destination*, consider the *weather* and decide *the length of time* you will stay on vacation.

Let us say you have a choice of going skiing in the mountains or going to an island resort.

On the island, you may plan daily excursions and plan to spend time at the beach, but it could rain. How will the weather affect your vacation?

Going skiing means that you are probably out on the mountain most of the day. Is there abundant snow where you are going? If it snows too much ("white out"), can you still go skiing?

If you decide to go skiing, you risk the chance of there being too much snow, so you need to have alternate plans if you cannot ski for a couple of days.

It is also important to know the length of time you will be on vacation to determine how much clothing to pack.

Now let's review how vacation planning compares to your asset allocation plan.

Your *investment objective* is like choosing a destination for your vacation; you must decide where you want your money to go.

The *amount of risk* you are willing to take is like planning for changes in the weather.

Time horizon is like the length of time you will be on vacation. When you invest, the length of time until you need the money points you to certain types of investments.

Diversification

The most important thing you can do when you invest is to spread your money around. This is called "diversification." Another term that we use for diversification is "asset allocation." Think of asset allocation as a baseball field with nine players in their respective positions and you are the manager.

The opposing team has hit the last four balls to centerfield. Would you reposition all your players to centerfield? Of course not: you want your players to stay in their positions, because you do not know where the other team will hit the ball next.

This analogy is just like investing. We do not know if large stock funds, small stock funds, international stocks or bonds will provide the most growth to our investments.

Remember the technology boom in the late 1990s. When technology stocks declined drastically in value, many people had all their money in technology stocks or mutual funds heavily invested in technology companies. When that did not work, they stopped putting money into the retirement plan or transferred it to money market funds. Then, when stocks recovered, they did not get the increased return because the money was in a money market fund earning almost nothing.

So position your investments just like baseball teams position their players: don't put all your investment "players" in the same asset "field."

Asset allocation will not always make you money. If stocks overall are declining in value, asset allocation may not fully protect you from losing some money, but try to remember that in a retirement plan you do not realize a loss unless you sell the funds.

Five Types of Investment Risk

There are five types of risk:
  1 Volatility or market risk
  2 Purchasing power or inflation risk
  3 Business specific
  4 Interest rate
  5 Accumulation

Volatility risk refers to the ups and downs in the value of your investments. Most people associate this with losing money. If you have a long-time horizon until you need the money, you can absorb more risk.

Purchasing power risk refers to the impact of inflation over time. You probably remember someone telling you how cheap things used to be when they were young: ten-cent postage stamps, 50-cent gas, automobiles for $1200 and homes for $25,000. Your investments need to keep up with inflation and that is why putting all your money in the money market or fixed account might cost you purchasing power later in life.

Business specific risk means your investment could decline rapidly in value if you invest in just one company. Mutual funds were developed to spread your money among many companies, but some mutual funds invest a majority of your money in similar companies. For example, if you are heavily invested in technology and that market sector loses favor all of a sudden, your investment will lose money. So goes the old saying, "Don't put all your eggs in one basket."

Interest rate risk: Most diversified portfolios have some money invested in bonds. If interest rates go up, bond values tend to drop. This is a problem for people who are more conservative with their money. Too much money in bonds as interest rates rise causes a loss in future purchasing power.

If you have a fixed account in your 401(k) plan, it is primarily invested in bonds. The investment company fixes the interest rate each year, or some contracts allow you to lock in a rate for 3, 5 or 10 years. If you lock in and rate and interest rates go up, you lose future purchasing power and you would have been better off in stocks or the money market.

Dollar Cost Averaging

Maybe someone will leave you some money or you owned a home in California, sold it, and moved to Montana, but if you do not save any money, you probably will not be able to retire comfortably. Any way you cut it, not having enough money is a drag. Thus, the most dangerous risk is the easiest to manage: just save more. Either start young with small amounts and do not touch it or increase your savings as you age.

One of the best ways to accumulate money is through a process called "Dollar Cost Averaging." Dollar Cost Averaging is built right into a 401(k) plan.

When you put money into mutual funds, you buy shares or units. Let us assume you invest $100 each pay period. In January, the mutual fund was selling at $10 a share/unit, so $100 bought 10 shares/units.

Then in February, the price drops to $5 per share/unit. Since the price is lower, your $100 investment purchased 20 shares/units. Now you own 30 shares/units with each being worth the current market price of $5, which means you have a loss of $50. (However, remember my earlier comment that the loss is not realized until you sell.)

Now we are into March and you find that the price is back to $10 per share/unit. You still are investing $100 so you buy 10 shares/units. Now you have 40 shares/units and they are worth $10, which means your account at the end of the quarter is worth $400. You have a $100 gain. Even though the investment is worth the same as it was in January you made money! Because you continued to invest while the price was down you were able to accumulate more shares/units. You bought the shares on sale!

Of course, this does not assure you of a profit if the stock market continues to decline and it can be disastrous if you only buy one stock because of the business risk, but when you have time on your side, it's a good idea to keep investing when the stock market goes down.

Risk Tolerance and Time Horizon

The next step is to determine your "risk tolerance" and "time horizon." When this is determined, you are placed in one of the following categories:
- Aggressive
- Moderately Aggressive
- Moderate (Balanced)
- Moderately Conservative
- Conservative

Each category has a stock, bond and cash allocation. For example, if you are young and are willing to take a lot of risk, your allocation under "aggressive" can be 90% stocks and 10% bonds. If you are older but can assume more risk, you can also be aggressive but your allocation may be 80% stocks and 20% bonds and cash. To cover every possible risk and time horizon, you would need 11 allocation models, as follows:

```
100% Stocks—   0% Bonds
 90% Stocks—  10% Bonds
 80% Stocks—  20% Bonds
 70% Stocks—  30% Bonds
 60% Stocks—  40% Bonds
 50% Stocks—  50% Bonds
 40% Stocks—  60% Bonds
 30% Stocks—  70% Bonds
 20% Stocks—  80% Bonds
 10% Stocks—  90% Bonds
  0% Stocks—100% Bonds
```

Within each of these allocations, there are assets classes, such as large cap, small cap, international securities, bonds and cash. Once most people establish a strategy, they rarely change their investments. This is called "buy and hold."

Buy and Hold

Once they determine what funds to invest in, most people never change their allocation. In the examples of different asset allocation strategies above, you can see there is a strategy for different risks and periods of time. These strategies are called "conservative," "moderate" and "aggressive." Once you have a strategy, you need to keep the same percentages that you started with because not adjusting your portfolio puts you at risk of losing more money than you bargained for because your portfolio is out of balance.

For example, if you choose to have 25% in international funds, 15% in mid cap, 10% in small cap, 40% in large cap and 10% in bonds, those percentages will change as time goes by because one style will make more money than another each year. Money should be moved between the funds to keep the same allocation. This is called "rebalancing" your portfolio.

Check with your investment provider because some will require you to do this online and others will allow you to have them do it for you. Your investment advisor should also be reviewing the funds with you and suggesting changes from time to time if the mutual fund(s) are no longer keeping up with their peers or appropriate benchmarks.

> *Buy and hold is a good strategy,*
> *but only if you rebalance and drop poor performing funds.*

If you know you need help and want someone to do the investing for you, I suggest hiring a "Registered Investment Advisor." Registered Investment Advisors (RIA's) are investment managers and use a strategy called "tactical" or "strategic" asset allocation. RIA's measure which asset style and what segment of our economy is the strongest. From this top-down analysis, they move your money where the most upside potential is or, in a bear market, into the style which offers the most safety. The tactical manager will move your money out of the stock market if the market is trending down where the strategic manager depends more on allocating your money across various asset styles.

Whether you do it yourself or hire someone to do it for you, you need to know your investment style.

Here is a quiz to determine your investment style.

Risk Tolerance Questionnaire

A Earning a high total return that will allow my invested capital to grow faster than the inflation rate is one of my most important objectives.

❏ Strongly Disagree (1 pt)
❏ Disagree (3 pts)
❏ Neutral (4 pts)
❏ Agree (5 pts)
❏ Strongly Agree (7 pts)

B The majority of my money is currently invested in:
   ❏ Savings or checking account (1 pt)
   ❏ Mutual funds/stocks or bonds (4 pts)
   ❏ Aggressive mutual funds/stocks (7 pts)

C I am willing to accept a potential short-term loss in return for a potentially higher long-term return.
   ❏ Strongly Disagree (1 pt)
   ❏ Disagree (3 pts)
   ❏ Neutral (4 pts)
   ❏ Agree (5 pts)
   ❏ Strongly Agree (7 pts)

D What is your primary investment goal?
   ❏ Maximize growth by obtaining highest total return on investment; current income is not a factor (7 pts)
   ❏ Obtain modest growth (5 pts)
   ❏ Stable return on investment while preserving most of my invested capital (3 pts)
   ❏ Avoid loss of initial investment value; current income is very important (1 pt)

E Which statement describes most accurately your tolerance to risk?
   ❏ I am willing to accept substantial declines in portfolio value in order to achieve my investment goals (7 pts)
   ❏ I can accept some declines in value in order to achieve my investment goals (4 pts)
   ❏ I am not willing to accept any loss in portfolio value in order to achieve my investment goals (1 pt)

Risk Tolerance Scoring: For each of your responses to the five questions above, please place the corresponding point value associated with your specific responses on the lines below:

A._____ B. _____ C. _____ D. _____ E. _____

TOTAL: _____

Scoring Key:
5–10 points   Conservative
11–16 points   Moderately Conservative
16–24 points   Moderate
23–28 points   Moderately Aggressive
24–35 points   Aggressive

Time Horizon

How long you have until retirement or when you need the money also determines how to invest. The closer you are to retirement, the less risky you may want to be. My feeling is that if for most of your career you were not very conservative, you should not all of a sudden become conservative. If you are too conservative, you may not be keeping up with inflation. This means you may run out of money. Adjust the time horizon accordingly.

How many years do you have until retirement?
• Less than 2 years
• 3 to 4 years
• 5 to 7 years
• 8 to 9 years
• More than 10 years

Identify Your Investor Profile

Find the place where your time horizon intersects with your risk tolerance score and circle your profile letter.

Find Your Investor Profile					
Time Horizon (in years)					
		10+	8-9	5-7	3-4	0-2
Risk Tolerance Score	29-35	A	MA	M	MC	C
	23-28	MA	MA	M	MC	C
	17-22	MA	M	M	MC	C
	11-16	M	MC	MC	MC	C
	5-10	MC	MC	C	C	C

(A= Aggressive MA= Moderately Aggressive M=Moderate MC=Moderately Conservative C=Conservative)

Sample Asset Allocation

Once you have found your investor profile, match it to the sample asset allocation model your investment provider illustrates in their enrollment materials. The following is a sample similar to what I have seen in enrollment guides.

Aggressive Portfolio	
International Stock Funds	20%
Small-Cap Stock Funds	15%
Mid-Cap Stock Funds	20%
Large-Cap Stock Funds	40%
Bond Funds	5%

Moderately Aggressive Portfolio

International Stock Funds	15%
Small-Cap Stock Funds	10%
Mid-Cap Stock Funds	15%
Large-Cap Stock Funds	40%
Bond Funds	10%
Cash Equivalents	10%

Moderate Portfolio

International Stock Funds	15%
Small-Cap Stock Funds	5%
Mid-Cap Stock Funds	10%
Large-Cap Stock Funds	30%
Bond Funds	25%
Cash Equivalents	15%

Moderately Conservative Portfolio

International Stock Funds	5%
Mid-Cap Stock Funds	15%
Large-Cap Stock Funds	30%
Bond Funds	30%
Cash Equivalents	20%

Conservative Portfolio

International Stock Funds	5%
Mid-Cap Stock Funds	15%
Large-Cap Stock Funds	20%
Bond Funds	35%
Cash Equivalents	25%

Asset Class Descriptions

International Stocks These stocks represent primarily the universe of non-US equity securities. Generally, mutual funds that invest no more than 49% in U.S. markets are classified as international stocks. Remember that international investing involves additional risks, including currency fluctuations, political instability and foreign regulations, all of which are magnified in emerging markets.

Small-Cap Stocks These stocks invest primarily in the stocks of smaller, lesser-known corporations that represent 80% of the smallest of the approximately 5000 domestic equity companies. Small-cap stocks have a higher growth potential but are also more volatile and have a greater probability of failing. Small-cap stocks involve increased risk and volatility.

Mid-Cap Stocks These stocks invest primarily in the stocks of mid-size corporations that represent about 15% of the 5000 domestic equity companies.

Large-Cap Stocks These stocks invest in the largest 5% of companies in the market. These are larger, more established, more profitable and well-known companies.

Bonds Bonds are issued by a corporation, the U.S. Government, or a governmental agency. A bond is a debt security and represents a loan. The loan is guaranteed to be repaid by a specified date with regular fixed interest payments.

Cash Equivalents Cash represents investments that generally do not fluctuate in market value and yield a regular interest payment. These investments might include bank deposits, money market, CDs and Treasury bills.

Summary

The asset allocation model shows how important it is to diversify your money. Most employee enrollment guides have examples or provide asset allocation portfolios. To invest in the correct portfolio you need to know the amount of risk you are willing to take and when you want your money. The more risk you are willing to take the more aggressive you want to be. Over extended periods, people have made more money investing in stocks than bonds. Bonds provide an income component where stocks tend to appreciate more over time.

For example, if you want pre-determined asset allocation portfolios commonly referred to as "lifestyle funds," you need to look at how the investment provider creates their portfolios. A lifestyle fund is a list of mutual funds that a professional has organized into a long-term investment strategy. Additionally there are managed portfolios that take advantage of economic indicators or trends and trade regularly (as opposed to lifestyle funds that generally buy and hold for an extended period). Without managed accounts or lifestyle funds, participants have to figure out where to put their money on their own.

ANNUAL RETURN FOR KEY ASSET CLASSES

	1994	1995	1996	1997	1998	1999	2000	2001	2002	2003	2004	2005	2006
Best	Foreign 7.78%	Large Growth 38.13%	Large Growth 23.97%	Large Growth 36.52%	Large Growth 42.16%	Small Growth 43.09%	Small Value 22.83%	Small Value 14.03%	Bonds 10.27%	Small Growth 48.53%	Small Value 22.25%	Foreign 13.54%	Foreign 26.34%
	Large Growth 3.14%	Large 37.58%	Large 22.96%	Large 33.36%	Large 28.58%	Large Growth 28.25%	Bonds 11.63%	Bonds 8.44%	Small Value -11.42%	Small 47.25%	Small 18.33%	Large 4.91%	Small Value 23.48%
	Large 1.32%	Large Value 36.99%	Large Value 22.00%	Small Value 31.78%	Foreign 20.00%	Foreign 26.96%	Large Value 6.08%	Small 2.49%	Foreign -15.94%	Small Value 46.02%	Small Growth 14.31%	Small Value 4.71%	Small Stocks 18.37%
	Small -1.81%	Small Value 25.75%	Small Growth 11.32%	Small Growth 12.93%	Small Growth 1.23%	Large Value 12.72%	Foreign -13.96%	Large -11.89%	Large -22.10%	Large 28.69%	Large 10.88%	Small 4.55%	Large 15.79%
	Small Growth -2.44%	Bonds 18.46%	Foreign 6.05%	Bonds 9.64%	Small -2.55%	Bonds -0.82%	Large Growth -22.08%	Large Growth -12.73%	Large Growth -23.59%	Large Growth 25.68%	Large Growth 6.13%	Large Growth 3.46%	Large Growth 11.01%
Worst	Bonds -2.92%	Foreign 11.21%	Bonds 3.64%	Foreign 1.78%	Small Value -6.46%	Small Value -1.48%	Small Growth -22.43%	Foreign -21.44%	Small Growth -30.27%	Bonds 4.11%	Bonds 4.34%	Bonds 2.43%	Bonds 4.33%

CHAPTER 9

Employee Education

PROPER EMPLOYEE EDUCATION ABOUT SAVING AND INVESTING IS SORELY LACK-
ING. One reason for this is that employers are reluctant to have meetings because they do not want to pay employees for time they are not working. They are also afraid to give investment advice. Additionally, some employees decide they do not want to be in the plan and want to skip the meeting. These people are a liability. They can later contend that they had no idea how important participating in the plan could have been and hold you responsible.

The materials offered by providers have improved greatly over the last few years. However, without the right people presenting the material, most employees do not comprehend the contents of their 401(k) enrollment brochure.

Holding an employee meeting needs to be a balanced affair: you need to engage the audience, teach them about how much money it takes to retire and how to invest. Too many meetings simply offer disclosures required by the government instead of teaching employees about savings and investing.

You should be telling your provider or financial advisor what you expect from the employee meeting. This is part of your fiduciary responsibility. If you have had a plan for a long time, you may want more technical investment education. If you are starting a plan, you may need more basic plan information so everyone understands how the plan works.

Here are some of the usual questions that employees want to know.

1 How does saving impact my paycheck?
2 When I retire, how long will my money last?
3 What does it mean to get tax-deferred earnings?
4 How do I get my money?
5 What happens if my employer goes bankrupt?
6 What about investing money after tax in a Roth account?
7 When can I change what I am deferring?
8 How do I review or change my investments?
9 Can I hire someone to invest my money?
10 Whom do I talk to if I have questions?
11 What costs am I incurring?
12 How does my 401(k) or profit sharing account statement translate into a monthly income at retirement?
13 How long will my money last after I retire?

The chapter on Investments can be the subject of an investment meeting all by itself. The paycheck comparison that follows is directed at your employees. It explains how money is taxed and when employees can get money from the plan. These are key factors helping employees both understand and feel good about their 401(k) plan.

How Your Paycheck is Affected

Why do you need a 401(k) when you can just stash some money under the mattress or at the bank?

Primarily because money put in a 401(k) plan comes out of your paycheck before you get a chance to spend it. Most working Americans do not have any money to save at the end of the month unless they save it up front. Additionally, you get a tax deduction immediately and the money (and any increase in the money) is tax deferred until you retire or leave your employer.

Let's compare an individual who has the choice of investing in a plan, the bank or does not save at all. Let's assume that he is a 30-year-old employee, single with one withholding, an annual income of $40,000, and he is paid over 24 pay periods:

Deferral %	0% paid into a 401(k) plan	5% paid into a 401(k) plan
Gross Pay	$1,666.67	$1,666.67
Pretax Deferral	$0	$133.33
Taxable Gross Pay	$1,666.67	$1,533.33
Social Security	$127.50	$127.50
Federal Tax	$221.00	$187.00
State Tax	$58.77	$48.10
NET AMOUNT	$1,259.40	$1,170.73
Deduction From Net	$0	$88.66
+ Tax Savings	$0	$44.67
+ Safe Harbor Match	$0	$66.67
Total Contribution	$0	$200.00
You're ahead by:	$0	$111.34

The chart above shows the effect on savings of putting money into a 401(k) plan. I am going to convert this to a monthly figure for further explanation.

Because you saved through the 401(k) plan, you have $222.68 more money a month overall. You are investing $400 a month, not just $266.66. There are two reasons for this: 1) You paid less tax, and 2) You got a company match.

What did it cost you to save $400 a month after taxes? It cost you $177.32 a month because you set money aside *before* it was taxed.

You will have to pay taxes when you take out the money, but you will have more money than trying to invest or save after taxes outside of a 401(k).

401(k) Balance @ Hypothetical 7.00% Interest

	No Plan	401(k)
After 5 years	$0	$29,536
After 10 years	$0	$70,961
After age 65	$0	$709,985

Notice that by not investing $400 a month for one year, *you will short yourself $51,248 at retirement!*

The point is to start saving when you are young.

How Long Will My Money Last?

Assumptions:

Amount of money at age 65:	$709,985.00
Monthly withdrawal	$4,000.00
Annual % increase	1%
Return on investment	6%
Marginal Tax Bracket	25%
Total amount of money accumulated	$1,139,663.00
Will last	22 years (or until 87 years old)

For example:

If you invest $400 a month for 35 years and earn 7%, you will accumulate $709,985. This means you can withdraw more than $50,000 a year for the rest of your life starting at age 65. You can also give the money to a top-rated insurance company and they will give you an annuity guaranteeing payments for life.

If you save $266.66 a month for 35 years and earn 4% (after taxes) in a savings account, you will accumulate approximately $244,000 or monthly payments of approximately $1,700 a month.

No Taxes Along the Way

There are no tax implications to buying and selling mutual funds through a 401(k) plan. All taxes are deferred until money is withdrawn. It is assumed you will take the money when you do not have other income, and the taxes you will pay at retirement are projected to be the same or lower than what you pay currently.

You did not have to pay taxes on the principle amount, capital gains, interest or dividends along the way. You are able to invest what the government would have otherwise taken in taxes. You pay taxes only for the year in which you take your money.

Think of it as your paycheck, except that you only need to pay federal tax and state tax (if your state has a tax). The result is that you will have more money saved than if you tried to save *after* taxes.

Background on Tax Advantages

The most appealing part of setting up a retirement plan is that all money contributed to the plan is *100% tax deductible*. This is true for the employees' contribution and any contributions an employer may make by means of matching contributions or pension/profit sharing contributions.

Employees that defer part of their pay receive an immediate tax break because no taxes are withheld from their pay. The money withheld from an employee's pay is transferred to investments provided by the 401(k) plan. In addition to the money going into the plan being excluded from your taxable income, you do not pay taxes on the growth of the money. The money is also *protected from creditors*.

Make Sure Your Plan is "Qualified"

If you end up in court owing money or declare bankruptcy, money in a qualified plan cannot be touched. The key word is "qualified" plan. If you end up in court saying your money can't be touched because it is in a retirement plan, that retirement plan had better be "qualified." "Qualified" means it has and is currently following all the rules and regulations imposed by government.

It is not uncommon to create circumstances that can cause a plan to not be considered "qualified" by our courts.

A Texas bankruptcy court went after the participant's account for settlement and won. The participant, who happened to be the only employee in the plan and owner of the company, was using plan money for his own benefit, such as for paying bills. This is a qualification issue. Although the IRS initially approved the plan, our court system doesn't have to follow the government's rulings.

Operationally you can do other things wrong because you didn't pay attention. There are many employers that do not amend their plans as required from time to time because of new laws. Failure to amend the plan means the plan is not qualified. You are not going to know if you have a qualification issue unless you have your plan audited every year.

Then there is divorce.

Divorce is a whole other topic for the courts. I could write a whole chapter on a requirement known as a Qualified Domestic Relations Order (QDRO), but I won't. The QDRO sets out how plan assets will be distributed. A plan may not distribute benefits unless it obtains a QDRO.

Roth 401(k)

I have shown you the immediate tax effect of saving inside a 401(k) plan. There is also an after-tax account called a Roth 401(k) that is a separate account under a traditional 401(k) plan. If you put money into the Roth account, you do not get a current tax break but you will not have to pay taxes when you withdraw the money at retirement.

Because the Roth account is not taxed when money is withdrawn, it may be a better choice for employees who believe they will be in a higher tax bracket when they retire. A Roth 401(k) account also avoids mandatory retirement distributions at age 70 ½ when you roll it over into an individual Roth account. (Mandatory distributions apply primarily to business owners, not rank-in-file employees.)

My feeling is that it is prudent to have both accounts. We do not know what the tax rates will be years from today, so having some taxable and non-taxable money makes sense.

By the way, your investment results will end up being the same if your tax bracket remains the same from now to retirement. Therefore, an after-tax saver is only better off if their tax bracket will be higher in the future.

Translating Lump Sum into Monthly Income

The best time to take your money is at retirement.

Employees usually ask the question, "how does my 401(k) or profit-sharing account statement translate into a monthly income at retirement?" The answer is found in how a defined benefit plan reports its benefit to plan participants. Defined Benefit plans are designed to provide a set amount of income per month upon reaching retirement age. Profit Sharing and 401(k) plans are designed to give a lump sum of cash. It is easier to relate to $500 a month upon retirement than an investment balance of $75,000.

I am starting to see 401(k) benefit statements that convert the lump sum to a projected monthly income at retirement so employees can see if they are meeting their retirement goals. However, you need to be careful when giving this advice because it is wholly determined on continuing to defer into the plan and earn the investment return you are currently receiving.

Getting Money Out of the Plan

Plan participants will pay taxes when they receive their money. There are seven ways to obtain a distribution or get money from a company-sponsored plan:

1 Termination of Employment
2 Retirement
3 Disability
4 Death
5 Hardship*
6 Plan Termination
7 In service distributions, usually after age 59 ½.
* *Hardship distributions cannot be rolled over to avoid current taxes.*

In each instance, the money is taxable unless transferred to another tax-deferred plan.

There is one more way to get your hands on some of the money without paying taxes: a "participant loan." Participants can borrow half of their vested account balance up to $50,000 without any tax consequences. Although you loan yourself the money, you must be repay it to yourself within five years. (A longer term [15 years] is available if the money is used to buy a home.)

Summary

In a nutshell, employees are eager to save money through their company's 401(k) plan because it comes out of their pay automatically, they have more to save because the money isn't taxed, and there is the potential of an employer matching contribution.

10

Complying with Regulation 404(c)

WHEN 401(K) PLANS WERE STARTING TO BECOME POPULAR, EMPLOYEES WERE NOT GIVEN THE OPTION TO INVEST THEIR OWN MONEY. The employer, with help from an investment advisor, created a portfolio of investments, and whatever that portfolio earned was divided up or allocated among all participants. This accounting method is known as "'balance forward."

An explanation of this concept will help you understand the downside to 404(c) plans and how the retirement plan providers are helping you to comply not only with 404(c) but with your fiduciary responsibility.

Let's first explain the "balance forward" accounting method and then see how most plans account for investments today.

Balance Forward Method

At the end of a specified period (generally quarterly or annually), the record keeper determines the gain or loss on the portfolio of investments and allocates earnings to the plan participants. This allocation is based on a predetermined formula or the most common method; the ratio of what each participant's account balance is to the total.

However, this is not an efficient way to manage a 401(k) plan because, 1) you only know the value of your account at the end of the year or per quarter, and 2) you must use the last valuation to sell securities when distributing money to terminated participants.

For example, if the value of the portfolio is X dollars on June 30th and you pay out money to the ex-employee on June 15th, the participant gets his share of X dollars as of June 30th, but the dollars may have a value less than X on June 15th. The rest of the portfolio takes the hit and the terminated participant comes out ahead. (Of course, the inverse is also true.)

This accounting procedure is still in place for many defined contribution plans. However, many plans use what is called "daily valuation" or "daily accounting." This means you know the account value every day and terminated employees receive exactly what their account is worth when receiving a distribution.

Daily Valuation

Mutual funds led the way to daily accounting. This is the system used to buy and sell securities. It was not long before the other purveyors of 401(k) plans that traditionally used the balance forward accounting began offer daily accounting.

When daily accounting became the standard, the next step was giving plan participants control of their own money. Instead of the employer creating an investment strategy or portfolio, now employees could create a strategy appropriate for their circumstance. This is called a "self-directed account."

Employers took the position that since they did not invest participant money, they were off the hook if the investments lost money. The problem with this is that the employer is a fiduciary and if employees do not invest prudently, the employer can still be held responsible.

To mitigate this dilemma, the employers can offer Fixed Accounts so employees will not lose any money. Employees not experienced at investing feel secure with an account that has a stated interest return, as opposed to the risks of the stock market.

Most employers offer a Fixed Account that guarantees principle and pays a predetermined interest rate. These accounts are similar in concept to the Certificates of Deposit (CD) banks offer. More than half of all the money invested in 401(k) plans ended up in fixed accounts from 1986 through most of the nineties, and, as you may recall, people investing in the stock market in the nineties made a lot of money.

Are You Offering Education?

If employers do not provide suitable education about long-term investing, do they breach their fiduciary responsibilities?

To help employers with this issue of fiduciary liability, the Dept of Labor offered a solution. The DOL created what is known as "non-fiduciary status for plan trustees and employers," called Regulation 404(c).

This regulation is not mandatory — that means you do not have to abide by it — but if you follow all the terms of Reg. 404(c), you achieve non-fiduciary status and cannot be sued if an employee's investment return turns out not as expected. (Caveat: If your investments are poor performing and have excessive fees, 404(c) may not be your savior.)

Here is what the DOL has to say on this issue.

> *In connection with the publication of the final rule regarding participant self directed individual account plans, the Department emphasized that the act of designating investment alternatives in an ERISA section 404(c) plan is a fiduciary function to which the limitation on liability provided by section 404(c) is not applicable. (DOL Advisory Opinion 98-04A)*

All that being said, I do not know of an employer who has not adopted 404(c). So let us see what you have to do to comply.

Requirements to Comply with 404(c)

1 Give an explanation of what 404(c) means and that the plan is intended to be a 404(c) plan.

2 A statement indicating that the named fiduciaries of the plan may be relieved

of liability for investment loses.

3 A description of the investment alternatives available under the plan.

4 A general description of the investment objective and risk and return characteristics of each designated alternative.

5 Identify any designated investment managers.

6 An explanation about giving investment instructions.

7 A description of any transaction fees and expenses, which affect the participant's, account balance.

8 The name, address and phone number of the plan fiduciary responsible for
providing plan information.

9 Specific information if employer stock is involved.

10 A copy of the most recent prospectus provided to the plan for investment alternatives subject to the Securities Act of 1933.

11 Any materials of voting, tender or similar rights.

12 Where the participant can obtain written confirmation of his investment
instructions.

13 The plan must permit participants to give investment instructions with a fre-
quency, which is appropriate in light of market volatility.

14 A core of investment alternatives constituting a broad range and permitting
the ability to change investments once every three months.

Additionally, the participant must be able to obtain upon request:

1 A description of the annual operating expenses of each investment alternative.

2 Copies of any prospectuses, financial statements, investment profiles and reports provided to the plan.

3 A list of the assets comprising the portfolio of each investment alternative.

4 Information concerning the value of shares or units of the investments offered.

5 Information concerning the value of shares or units in the investments held
in the accounts of the participant.

You will not find this information in any one place in your plan documentation,
so you will find it difficult to ascertain whether you comply.

Most 401(k) providers will tell you their materials comply with 404(c), but it
is *your responsibility* to make the information available.

For example, if you are required to provide participants with a prospectus when they enroll, that might be easy. Just have them available after each
employee meeting. However, what if a participant changes investments along

the way? Chances are you do not even know (or care) that one of your people changed funds, so how could you comply and send them a prospectus?

Some commentators have said that you only need to make a prospectus available if a participant asks for one. Prospectuses are available online as are investment profiles explaining the fund. However, making prospectuses available does not mean your participant received one.

Securities laws (under the rules of the Securities and Exchange Commission [SEC]) say a stockbroker cannot sell you a fund if a prospectus isn't included. The SEC does not control 401(k) plans, but you are at risk of not complying with 404(c) if a participant does not receive the proper disclosures.

Where does the participant find information about the fee, commission, and expenses of each mutual fund? If you are in an insurance company packaged plan, you will not find it in the prospectus. In fact, the prospectus is not the recommended format for determining these costs.

Luckily, top insurance companies provide an "Investment Profile." This is a one-page summary generally referred to as a Morningstar or Standard & Poor's report. Even then, you may not find the underlying asset management fees the insurance charges to compensate them for providing their services and that of their broker.

404(c) Best Practices

First, understand that 404(c) compliance is not easy. Second, the rule says you must comply with *all* 404(c) requirements, and third, if you should be sued, the court may rule against you even if you have intended to comply but failed to procedurally.

Best practice is to do everything you can to comply with 404(c).

Second, if you do not fully comply it is unlikely that you will be sued. As a good fiduciary, you should have an investment policy, monitor the funds, review expenses and remove inferior funds. In other words, if you are a good fiduciary, participants will not have any grounds to sue you.

Summary

I began this chapter with the concepts of balance forward and daily accounting. This was so you could gain some understanding of 401(k) accounting. Then when employers found out they could avoid investment liability, they passed the responsibility of investing onto the participants, which is called "self-directed accounts."

However, after realizing that participants did not have the knowledge to properly invest for their future, employers offered managed accounts. True managed accounts trade based upon strategic or tactical research.

Other accounts are called "lifestyle" or "target maturity" funds. These funds are not actively managed but do rebalance and look to maintain quality managers.

In other words, we are practically back to where it all began, offering portfolios of funds chosen by the employer to make available to plan participants. The modernization factor is that instead of one portfolio in the plan, we have several, from conservative all-bonds and cash to aggressive all equities.

If you want a manager who actively manages your money, you should hire an RIA. (See Chapter II on "Parties to the Plan.") The plan trustee can hire an RIA to take on the responsibility of choosing investments for plan participants. When an employer hires an RIA, he transfers the liability to that manager. Now all the employer has to do is see to it that the manager does as well as other managers, an easier task than monitoring all the funds in the 401(k) plan.

Next we will discuss the "Plan Document."

CHAPTER 11

The Plan Document

PART OF THE SERVICE YOU SHOULD EXPECT TO RECEIVE FROM YOUR PROVIDER IS PLAN DOCUMENT ASSISTANCE. Plan documentation involves completing a legal plan document that is approved by the Internal Revenue Service (IRS). Without a legal plan document, you are not entitled to the tax deferred growth and tax deductions offered by the government.

Plan documentation involves determining who is eligible, when participants get distributions, if loans are permitted, what to do with non-vested money.... and the list goes on. Adding more cost and confusion to maintaining a plan is the requirement that you *must* amend the plan document as laws change. (Be sure your provider is keeping your plan up-to-date! The IRS is very serious about plan sponsors having a proper plan document.)

The plan document has all the rules you must follow to protect participants and beneficiaries, but if you read the plan document, you will quickly conclude that you need help deciphering all the terms and procedures the government requires. This is where an Attorney or TPA schooled in the laws and regulations found in the Internal Revenue Code (usually referred to as the ERISA law) can help you.

Most employers assume that their provider — be it a TPA, investment company or attorney — will keep their plan in compliance.

> *Do not assume your plan is in compliance!*
> *Ask your provider or attorney annually*
> *if there are any changes in laws*
> *that affect the operation of your plan*
> *and if you need to do something about it*
> *or if you can take advantage of the new rules.*

There are rules that must be stated in this document that may have no bearing on your situation, but they are required to be in your plan document. Additionally, the government from time to time requires you to adopt amendments to the plan that may have nothing to do with how you operate your plan. A word to the wise: Do not ignore these amendments! The government requires all plans to have provisions they deem appropriate. Part of the Plan you can design; other parts are imposed on you.

A well-designed plan contains instructions (also known as plan provisions, procedures or language) on how your plan is to be operated. Additionally, the government imposes many operating instructions that may or may not affect you. A well-designed plan has provisions or procedures specific to your circumstances. In addition, a well-designed plan may purposefully not be specific in certain areas, and this can afford flexibility when used appropriately. A plan document designed for you will allow for consistent management of plan details and make the plan easier to maintain.

What Can Go Wrong?

Most plans have a one-page summary or plan highlights that are made available to participants and used by your in-house administrator. It is not unusual that these highlight pages do not get updated along with amendments to the plan document. This means the plan is probably not operating in accordance with the plan document.

If the document is not followed or properly maintained, the plan can be disqualified and then all the money becomes taxable. Disqualification is rare, however.

Instead, the IRS will penalize you. Penalties can add up to thousands of dollars plus the cost to prepare all necessary paperwork the government will require.

Parts of the Plan Document

The part of the document that describes the terms of the program, such as who is eligible, what contributions can be made, how service is calculated, what limitations the plan has, etc., is called the *Plan*. The party that takes title to the money deposited with the investment company or mutual fund is governed by the *Trust*.

The purpose of a Trust is to take title to the money for the benefit of the participants or the participants' beneficiary. The Trust is a separate legal entity that enables you to segregate the money from your company. Note: The law says that if the money is in a qualified Trust, it is protected from creditors.

There may also be a third document often associated with prototype plans, called an *Adoption Agreement*. You can design the variables in a plan by checking off the boxes on the Adoption Agreement that coordinate with the Plan and Trust document.

Amend the Plan When Required

Retirement laws seem to change constantly. Be sure to keep your plan up-to-date. The downside of not amending it is that your provider may not be giving you all the options currently available.

On a practical basis, the TPA or organization doing the compliance and government reporting for you may be operating the plan in accordance with current law but not amending the plan until later. This is permissible and a valid procedure due to the government not coming out with regulations that allow attorneys and document providers to come up with the correct language for the plan document that the government deems appropriate. Therefore, it is a timing issue dealing with the document updating process. Expect to pay extra to keep your plan document up-to-date.

However, just signing another Adoption Agreement because an investment company hands them out free is dangerous. For example, I was introduced to an employer that for years vested their employees based on the date the employee entered the plan. When the law changed requiring restating the plan in its entirety, they took a short cut and signed a new plan document with their investment provider. The new document provided vesting from the date an employee was hired, which is a usual standard.

However, when I read the new plan, it was obvious a change had occurred that was not being followed. The problem was that the employer was giving less credit to terminated employees than the plan said it should, a serious violation. Although it was unintended, the employer had to go back to every employee that terminated employment to give them one more year of credit and the corresponding amount of money they were shorted. What really made the job time consuming and expensive was going back to correct distributions for three years of terminated employees.

A "Qualified Plan"

Without the required legal plan documents properly completed, you do not have a "qualified plan," which means a company-sponsored retirement plan permitting you and your employees to take current tax deductions and accumulate money on a tax-deferred basis.

Providers, Attorney's and TPA's have obtained approval from the Internal Revenue Service to sponsor plan documents. When you sign the plan document, you immediately have a "qualified plan," but there are issues that could negate this qualification in the future.

You must follow the plan's terms. Common violations involve bringing an ineligible employee into the plan, excluding an eligible employee, not counting bonuses as part of pay for contribution purposes, exceeding limits for contributions and calculating years of service incorrectly (as referred to above in the case of the employer that had their plan restated but didn't follow the plan).

The Internal Revenue Service (IRS) says you have a qualified plan when you adopt plans called "Volume Plans" or "Prototype Plans." However, if the plan has special provisions (such as combinations of formulas that favor highly paid employees, excluding a class of employees), you may want the protection of having a letter from the IRS that says the plan was completed properly and that if you follow the plan the IRS cannot disqualify the plan on audit. For this reason, it's wise to apply to the IRS for what is called a "Determination Letter," which is like an insurance policy.

Fewer employers are applying for these determination letters because they feel that, since the plan is already approved, they do not need their own approval.

This is a matter of personal preference. I recommend the Determination Letter process because it shows the IRS you are holding yourself to a higher standard, and if you have special provisions or circumstances, the letter is your insurance that if the plan was operated according to the plan document it will remain a "qualified plan."

To give you an idea of the procedures involved in a 401(k) plan, here is a typical plan document Table of Contents with an explanation of what each term means.

Sample Plan Document Table of Contents

ARTICLE 1 — DEFINITIONS

Contains definitions of terms. (Anytime these headings appear in the document they are capitalized, so you know you can go to Article 1 to determine their meaning.)

ARTICLE 2 — PLAN PARTICIPATION

Explains eligibility to participate in the various aspects of the plan — deferrals, match and non-elective (profit sharing)

ARTICLE 3 — CONTRIBUTIONS AND ALLOCATIONS

Explains deferral, match and non-elective contributions and how they will be allocated to participants

ARTICLE 4 — PLAN BENEFITS

Explains when benefits are paid out at death, disability, retirement and termination of employment

ARTICLE 5 — DISTRIBUTION OF BENEFITS

Explains the form in which benefits are paid out at death, disability, retirement and termination of employment

ARTICLE 6 — CODE SECTION 415 LIMITATIONS

Explains Code Section 415 limits on accounts and top heavy rules

ARTICLE 7 — DUTIES OF THE TRUSTEE
>   Explains the appointment, scope, duties, change of trustee

ARTICLE 8 — DUTIES OF THE PLAN ADMINISTRATOR
>   The Plan Administrator is the Sponsoring Employer and this
>   section outlines powers and duties.

ARTICLE 9 — AMENDMENT, TERMINATION AND MERGER
>   Explains the process for plan amendment, termination or
>   merger

ARTICLE 10 — MISCELLANEOUS PROVISIONS
>   Covers titling, bonding, legal action, limitations on liability, etc.

12

Eligibility and Vesting

THE PLAN DOCUMENT DEFINES WHO IS ELIGIBLE TO MAKE SALARY DEFERRALS INTO THE 401(K) PLAN.

Eligibility Details

Every retirement plan has eligibility provisions. They are often referred to as the "waiting period."

In a 401(k) plan, the maximum waiting period is one year from date of hire with entry dates no less than semi-annually and a minimum age requirement of 21 years old.

They are many ways to slice and dice eligibility. Here are some common waiting periods:

• No eligibility or zero eligibility

- Three Months
- Six Months
- One Year

Most plans limit participation to participants with a minimum age of 21 because employees under 21 generally don't participate. If you have many people under age 21 who do not intend to participate, this can create additional administrative expense and can cause the plan to fail non-discrimination testing issues.

What Can Go Wrong?

It is common for employers to assume that part-time employees or employees who do not sign up are ineligible, but the government reporting and compliance requirements require *all* eligible employees be part of general and non-discrimination testing. Generally, any employee who works 1000 hours a year and receives a W-2 should be treated as eligible, after the waiting period, unless specifically excluded by the terms of the plan.

Do not assume that leased employees, contract labor or employees of other entities you own are excluded.

Reduce the Risk of Non-compliance

No less often than annually provide your third party administrator with a list of all employees employed during the year along with their dates of birth, hire dates, termination dates, hours worked and compensation for the plan year. Request they test the plan with all this information.

Should I Have a Minimum Age Requirement?

If you do not generally hire employees under 21, a minimum age requirement is not necessary. If do you have employees under age 21, ask them if they want to contribute to the plan. If most want the plan, don't have a minimum age requirement. If you have many employees under age 21 and most do not want to contribute or do not contribute because their wages tend to be around the minimum wage, a minimum age requirement is a good idea.

Entry Date

In conjunction with the eligibility period, you need an Entry Date. If you just said that everyone has to wait one year to get in the plan, you would have 365 entry dates. Too many entry dates just means you have to follow up more often so no one is left out. The three most popular entry dates are:

- The first day of the next calendar quarter after you meet the eligibly requirement
- A semi-annual date six months after you meet eligibility requirement. (Twice a year)
- The first of the month after meeting eligibility requirement

Monitor Eligibility

It is the employer's responsibility to monitor the eligibility requirements (unless your provider has agreed to do it for you). You will get in trouble if you have a matching contribution or make an elective contribution (employer paid) and you leave out an otherwise eligible employee. This is considered discrimination in operation and can get you fined or even have the plan disqualified.

Your provider will ask you to provide a listing of all your employees, either along the way or at the end of the Plan Year (the twelve-month period under which you operate the plan, usually the calendar year). From this payroll data, they do non-discrimination testing and should check to be sure you have not added someone who was not eligible or left someone out who was eligible.

You should set up a procedure at year-end to send to the administrator who is responsible for your testing an electronic spreadsheet detailing all your employees for the plan year with each employee's name, social security number, date of birth, date of hire, and compensation. Ask them in writing to test eligibility. (Most services which manage 401[k] plans do not test for eligibility because they are either not contracted to do so or the Employer does not provide census data.)

Providers have so many of these year end tests to do that it is difficult to get the information done in a timely manner if you don't get them your data promptly.

Unfortunately, most small employers do not want to take the extra time to compile employee census data with the result that they create a serious breach of fiduciary liability by not providing the necessary data to do compliance testing at year-end. (Interestingly, I have seen employers fire their provider to save face, claiming the provider should have been more on top of them to be sure the data was sent!)

If you have a retirement plan, you should be sending all the information the provider needs to do the compliance work as soon as possible after the plan year closes.

Who Has to Participate?

Generally, all employees who meet the eligibility requirements enter the plan. I have had employers tell me that they did not believe they could have a plan unless a certain number of employees agreed to participate, but there are no minimum participation requirements for defined contribution plans such as 401(k) or profit sharing plans.

In some instances, employers have a need to exclude certain people, departments or divisions. You can even offer different levels of benefits. If you have a safe harbor 401(k) plan, the HCE's can save up to the dollar limit even if no NHCE's participate.

To comply with coverage requirements, you must pass either the Percentage Test or the Average Benefits Test.

The Percentage Test

To satisfy the percentage test, a plan must cover at least 70% of the NHCE's as a ratio to the HCE's. For example, if you have 30 employees of which three are HCE, you must cover at least 70% of 27 (i.e., 19). If one of your HCE's is excluded, the ratio changes to at least 46% of 27 (i.e., 15).

This plan design technique can help reduce the cost of covering certain employees, but it requires constant testing and should be done by organizations such as those a TPA sets up to help you oversee the "Coverage and Participation" testing requirements. Also, be sure the plan document spells out who is not being covered, even though the law allows you exclude a certain percent of your workforce.

The Average Benefits Test

To satisfy the average benefits test, the benefits provided to NHCE's must be at least 70% as great, on average, as benefits provided to the HCE's. These benefit percentages may be determined on either a contributions or a benefits basis.

Unfortunately, the math on this calculation exceeds the scope of my book. You just need to know that excluding employees or providing different levels of benefits or contributions is possible.

Vesting

The portion of an employee's account in a retirement plan that is "vested" belongs to the employee. The vested portion cannot be reclaimed by the employer. The portion not vested is forfeited upon termination of employment. Forfeited money can either be redistributed to all participants or used by the employer to reduce future employer contributions. The employer must choose one method and it must be stated in the plan document.

Employees are immediately 100% vested in their own salary deferral contributions. For employer contributions, the employer has limited options to delay the vesting of their contributions to the employee. For example, the employer can say that the employee must work with the company for three years or they lose any employer contributed money, which is known as "cliff vesting."

The most poplular vesting schedule is called 2-20. If you leave the plan after one year, you forfeit 100% of the company's money but in the second and succeeding years you accrue 20% per year. The schedule looks like this:

Years of Service	Vested Percentage
1	0
2	20
3	40
4	60
5	80
6	100

Choosing a vesting schedule allows an employer to reward employees who remain employed for several years. In theory, this allows the employer to make greater contributions than would otherwise be prudent, because the money they contribute on behalf of employees goes to the ones they most want to reward.

Years of Service

The general rule is all years of service with the employer must be counted towards vesting. For example, if you have a one-year eligiblity period, an employee would have two yeas of credited service after being in the plan for only one year.

When it comes to counting years of service for retirement plans, a "year" is defined as a twelve-month period in which a participant works 1000 hours. There are 2080 hours in a year if you work 40 hours a week. Therefore, about half way through each year a participant moves up the vesting schedule.

Monitoring Investments

A. Overview

The Employer or Investment Committee will periodically monitor and evaluate the specific investment alternatives to determine if they continue to be suitable and appropriate for the Plan and the participants.

B. Fund Monitoring

1 The Employer or Investment Committee will periodically obtain reports for all Funds, which include a full and comprehensive review and evaluation of each Fund with respect to the portfolio and performance standards in this IPS. The Employer or Investment Committee will meet at appropriate inter-

vals to review this Investment Policy Statement, the investment structure and the investment alternatives offered by the Plan.

2 A fund will be expected to maintain an overall rating in the 2nd quartile (above median). (Funds above the second quartile are in the top 50% of all funds). However, if a Fund is rated below average for a length of time as determined by the Employer or Investment Committee this will normally not be cause for the removal of the Fund. If a Fund is rated below average for four or more quarters it will normally, but not necessarily, be removed by the Investment Fiduciary. If a fund is removed, the Employer or Investment Committee will normally replace the Fund with similar fund, using the procedures in this IPS for the selection of a fund. However, the Employer or Investment Committee may determine that a removed Fund will not be replaced.

3 If a Fund is removed for future contributions, the following procedures will generally be followed by the Employer or Investment Committee:

a The monies will ordinarily be transferred to the replacement Fund, if the Employer or Investment Committee selects one. Alternatively, the Employer or Investment Committee may inform the participants of its intention to remove the Fund and permit the participants to direct the transfer of their monies from the Fund being removed. In that case, the Employer or Investment Committee will transfer any monies remaining in that Fund at the time of its removal to the replacement Fund, if one is selected. Otherwise, the monies will be transferred to the most appropriate investment alternative, as determined by the Employer or Investment Committee.

b The Employer or Investment Committee may implement reasonable procedures, including blackout periods, to accomplish these changes.

C. Monitoring of Asset Allocation Funds

The Employer or Investment Committee will periodically obtain and review information necessary to determine whether the asset allocation funds are performing in a manner consistent with the objectives of the IPS.

Designated Funds and Benchmarks

As of the effective date of this Investment Policy Statement (IPS), the Designated Funds and their respective benchmarks are:

Asset Class	Fund Name	Market Index	Peer Group
Cash		SB 3-month T-Bill Index	S&P Money Market Taxable
Bonds		LB Aggregate Bond Index	S&P Fixed Income General Intermediate
Large-Cap Stocks		S&P 500, S&P/ BARRA 500 Value or S&P/ BARRA 500 Growth Index, depending on the fund selected	S&P Equity Large-Cap Value or Growth, depending on the fund selected
Mid-Cap Stocks		Russell Mid-Cap, Russell Mid-Cap Value, or Russell Mid-Cap Growth Index depending on the fund selected.	
Small-Cap Stocks		Russell 2000, Russell 2000 Value or Russell 2000 Growth Index, depending on the fund selected	S&P Equity Small-Cap Value or Growth, depending on the fund selected

International Developed Equity		MSCI EAFE Index or MSCI Emerging Markets Free Index, depending on the fund selected	S&P Equity International or S&P Equity Emerging Markets, depending on the fund selected

Fund Evaluation Measures

Each fund is evaluated based on six evaluation measures (fund evaluation measures) that quantify the relative operating expenses, total returns and risk-adjusted performance of a fund within its peer group. The total returns of cash equivalents and index funds are evaluated against their specific market benchmarks. The evaluation methodology is not an attempt to predict a fund's future potential; it summarizes how well each fund has historically balanced expenses, returns and risk. The six evaluation measures together provide a systematic process to evaluate and monitor funds using generally accepted investment principles and modern portfolio theories.

Short-term Measures
- *Expense Ratio* (current) peer group ranking
- *Sharpe Ratio* (trailing 36-month) peer group ranking

Intermediate-term Measures
- *Trailing Performance* (3-year, 5-year and 10-year annualized total returns; weighted) peer group ranking
- *Information Ratio* (36 rolling 36-month information ratios) peer group ranking

Long-term Measures
- *Performance Consistency* (rolling 12-month total returns for the past 10 years) peer group ranking
- *Style Selection Return* (rolling 36-month style selection returns for the past 10 years) peer group ranking

Additional Warning Signs

The following criteria should be evaluated to determine potential risks and provide information to assist the Investment Fiduciary in making prudent investment decisions.

- **High operating expenses**

  Rank each fund within its peer group on based on recent operating expense data. Review funds that have an operating expense ratio above the peer group average.

- **High individual holding concentration**

  Review funds with more than 10% of assets in any one stock, or more than 50% of assets in the top ten holdings.

- **High economic sector concentration**

  Review funds with more than the greater of 25% of assets or 1.5 times the peer group average sector weight in any one economic sector.

- **High portfolio turnover**

  Rank each equity fund within its peer group by portfolio turnover. Flag the funds in each equity peer group with portfolio turnover in the highest 10% of their peer group.

- **Low style purity**

  Rank each equity fund within its peer group by correlation with the market benchmark assigned to the fund's S&P style classification. Regress each equity fund's monthly returns against the monthly returns of its corresponding market benchmark using a single 36-month trailing period computation. Review equity funds within the lowest 10% of R-squared for each peer group.

- **High duration bet**

  Review bond and hybrid funds with a 3-year average return 1.5 or more years above or below the 3-year average duration of the peer group.

- **Low credit quality average**

  Review bond and hybrid funds with a current average credit rating below" A."

- **Low manager tenure**
Review funds whose portfolio managers have less than one year of tenure managing the fund.

- **Low asset base**
Flag funds with less than $50 million in assets.

Summary

The IPS:

1 States objectives, restrictions, and general investment structure for management of plan assets.
2 Provides the basis for evaluating the plan's results.
3 Helps communicate plan investment guidelines and procedures to other advisors and participants.
4 Provides direction for making future investment decisions.

14

Simple IRA Plans for Small Businesses

IN 1997, THE SIMPLE IRA WAS ESTABLISHED SO THAT SMALL BUSINESSES COULD HAVE AN EFFECTIVE, COST-EFFICIENT WAY TO OFFER RETIREMENT BENEFITS TO THEIR EMPLOYEES. This type of plan is targeted at businesses of 100 employees or less that offer no other retirement savings plan. If, in a subsequent year, you exceed 100 employees, you have two years to terminate the plan. Very small companies often start with a SIMPLE IRA and move to the more versatile 401(k) plan.

Eligibility

Employees who are 21 years or older and have been employed for at least a year can be eligible to participate in this plan.

Employer Contributions

Employers have two options for contribution. The first contribution method encourages employee participation by requiring the employer to match all employee contributions up to 3% of their salaries. The 3% is calculated on total compensation, with no limitation (as there is with a 401[k] plan).

The second option is a fixed contribution plan. In this case, employers pay a flat 2% of a worker's salary. This contribution is required for all participating employees, regardless of whether the employees contribute on their own.

COMPARISON OF SIMPLE IRA PLANS VS. TRADITIONAL PLANS

SIMPLE IRA plans are less expensive.

Since the SIMPLE IRA is not subject to the stringent discrimination tests that apply to traditional 401(k) plans, the annual costs of administering the plan tend to be substantially reduced.

SIMPLE IRA plans have lower employee contribution limits.

SIMPLE IRA plans have lower maximum employee contribution limits than traditional 401(k) plans. For instance, the maximum that an employee can contribute to a SIMPLE IRA for 2007 is $10,500 plus $2,500 catch up; the maximum employee contribution in a 401(k) is $15,500, plus $5,000 catch up contribution.

SIMPLE IRA plans require mandatory employer contributions.

SIMPLE IRA plans require employers to make contributions to their employees' accounts. Employer contributions are optional for traditional 401(k) plans.

SIMPLE IRA plans have automatic vesting of employer contributions.

Employer contributions made to SIMPLE IRA plans are automatically fully vested. Traditional 401(k) plans, in comparison, provide employers the option of creating vesting schedules, whereby employer contributions become fully vested over a period of years.

15

A Simplified Employee Pension Plan (SEP)

WHEN A SMALL EMPLOYER WANTS TO PROVIDE A TAX-DEFERRED SAVINGS PLAN FOR ITS EMPLOYEES, THERE ARE SEVERAL CHOICES, ONE OF WHICH REQUIRES NO GOVERNMENT REPORTING. It is called a "SEP" (short for "Simplified Employee Pension Plan").

An SEP is a glorified IRA (Individual Retirement Account) for employees of a business entity: all the employer contributions are held in an IRA that allows for higher contribution limits. The Employer can tax defer for each eligible employee the lesser of 25% of compensation or $44,000 (as adjusted for cost of living from time to time). What the business owner does for him-/herself he/she must do for his/her employees as a percentage of taxable wages. If the owner saves 15%

of taxable wages then 15% must be done for other eligible employees.

The IRA-based SEP Plan has *three advantages* over the more popular Profit Sharing Plan.

1 There is no cost to set up and administer the plan.
2 The plan can be set up as late as the employer's tax filing due date (plus extensions).
3 There is no government filing requirement.

However, the *disadvantages* will make the SEP more costly than the Profit Sharing Plan (PSP) if you have more than a few employees.

While in a PSP you can exclude employees working fewer than 1000 hours a year, in an SEP, you must cover employees if they earned $450 in the year. SEP eligibility is three years (technically, if an employee worked three out of the last five years) where in a PSP the eligibility period cannot exceed two years, and one year if the plan has 401(k) provisions.

Although eligibility is faster in PSP, you can have a vesting schedule where an SEP requires 100% immediate vesting.

If owners and other highly compensated employees have money under the plan that equals 60% of all the money in the plan, the plan is considered "top heavy." A top-heavy plan requires the business to contribute 3% of all eligible employee wages to the plan.

In a PSP you can require that employees be employed on December 31st while a SEP requires a contribution once they have met eligibility and earned $450.

There are no loan provisions but employees can withdraw money at any time from an SEP. This is both an advantage and disadvantage. The employee can get their hands on their money and must include it with any other money they earned and pay taxes come April 15th. There is also a 10% excise tax if you are under age 59 1/2.

Sometimes it may be advantageous to add a 401(k) plan. However, you cannot have another plan, such as a 401(k), unless your SEP is individually designed. This means you can't use a pre-packaged plan. (You can tell a plan is a packaged plan because they have you sign a form produced by the IRS called a Form 5305-SEP.)

You have until the due date (including extensions) of the employer's tax return to establish an SEP. A Profit Sharing Plan must be established by the end of the employer's fiscal year but does not have to be funded until the due date of the tax return plus extensions.

16

The Defined Benefit Plan

THE DEFINED BENEFIT PLAN IS A PENSION PLAN. A pension plan is a program that provides income for employees that they can not out live. This is a good deal if you can get it. Work for a company until retirement and walk away with approximately 30% of your salary forever. (You can have a plan that offers 100% of your salary at retirement but most large plans offer around 30%). For the average worker 30% from your company plus what you get from social security means you are retiring with 90% of your current income.

The 401(k) plan is only guaranteed based on what you and your employer contribute to the plan. The defined benefit plan does not require employee contributions and is completely paid for by the employer.

Your 401(k) plan statement generally tells you how much money you have but not what that lump of cash means in terms of monthly income at retirement.

It's easier to relate to $500 a month upon retirement than an investment balance of $75,000. While Profit Sharing and 401(k) Plans are designed to give you a lump sum of cash, a Defined Benefit Plan is a company-sponsored retirement plan that is designed to provide you with a stream of monthly payments for as long as you live, and, if you are married, for as long as your spouse lives. (Another term for monthly payments from a retirement plan is a "pension," or, as I like to call it, a paycheck you cannot outlive.)

From an Employer's perspective, the cost of the plan is determined by the paycheck he wants to give to his employees. A typical pension plan might call for a pension of 30% of your salary. Therefore, when you retire at age 65, the plan owes you one-third of your pay.

How Much Money Do I Need to Save?

Let us say you are the owner and only employee of your company. You are 50 years old and will retire in 15 years. Your goal is to have $7,500 a month when you retire and you want it to last for as long as you live. How much money do you have to save to accumulate enough cash to pay yourself $7,500 a month forever? (Let us assume you will earn 6% interest compounded annually.)

The answer is that will you need to save $43,000 a year in order to accumulate one million dollars. I know this because insurance companies have determined, based on interest and mortality calculations, that anyone age 65 who gives them one million dollars can receive from them $7,500 a month for life (give or take a few dollars, depending upon the insurance company).

In other words, in a Defined Benefit Pension, you determine either how much money you want at retirement and save whatever it takes to get there or you have a budget that determines how much pension you will create. For example, in the above illustration, you saved $43,000 to get $7,500 a month; if you save $60,000, you could receive $10,500 a month.

What if I Have Employees?

The next question is, what happens if I have employees? In that case, the cost of the plan will depend on how much pension you need and that formula is applied to all the other employees eligible to be in the plan. For example, if you have a 30-year-old employee earning $36,000 a year, the cost to provide a monthly pension of 50% of their pay at age 65 is $1,800 a year.

Note: I am starting to see 401(k) benefit statements that convert the money in their account to a projected monthly income at retirement so employees can see if they are meeting their retirement goals. However, you need to be careful when giving this advice because it is wholly dependent on continuing to defer into the plan and earn the investment return you are currently receiving.

Defined Benefit Plans will cost more if you are older and less if you are younger. The more time you have until retirement, the more time you have to put your money to work. This is the magic of compound interest.

What if I Die Before I Use Up My Savings?

The question I always get after this explanation is, "What happens if I die before I use up the million?" The answer depends on the deal you make with the Defined Benefit Plan or the insurance company.

You can ask them to refund the balance or guarantee payments for 10 years or 15 years. They could also pay you a lesser amount and continue making payments after your death to your spouse, which is called a "joint and survivor annuity."

Guarantees offered by insurance companies will reduce your monthly payments, but if you believe you will live a long time, locking in the guarantee will be worth more if you live a long time.

Although the plan is based on you receiving a stream of payments for life, which we call a "pension" or "annuity," you can also convert the pension to cash. It is usually best to take the pension and spread out the taxes due; then you will only be taxed on the amount you receive.

If you are married, retirement plan regulations set forth by the government suggest you take the annuity as a "joint and survivor annuity." This means when you die your spouse will continue to receive benefits for as long as he or she lives.

There are many possible payout variations. How you will receive the money does not have to be determined until you retire, terminate employment or when the employer stops the plan and distributes the money to all participants.

To summarize: If you want to guarantee a stream of payments guaranteed, it is best to transfer the money in the plan to an insurance company. Insurance companies can guarantee the payments and you do not have to rely upon yourself or an advisor to prudently invest the money. However, you should also consider weighing this option against a portfolio designed for you by a registered investment advisor. And you can do some of both; annuity and investment portfolio.

The Plan can also make payments according to a schedule based on interest and mortality. This requires the Trustees (generally the business owner) to properly manage the assets to guarantee that the plan does not run out of money. Most Trustees hire an investment manager to assist them in investing the money. However, only insurance companies are approved to offer a lifetime benefit on a guaranteed basis.

Summary

A defined benefit plan provides a pension at some point in the future. While all other types of plans are based on how much money is saved and how much it earns, the Defined Benefit Plan is guaranteed. Naturally, the Employer must maintain the plan for the employee to get the full benefit. If the plan is terminated, the employees will get whatever they have accrued. (I will expand on this issue later.) The target is generally retirement age as defined by the plan, which is usually 65, but it could be any age appropriate for your situation.

More Details (if you like math)

How large is the benefit at retirement?
The maximum pension depends on your age, your length of time until retirement and your compensation history. The maximum you can obtain as of this writing is a pension of $175,000 a year at age 65. This amount is adjusted by the cost of living from time to time. This means that at age 65 you will have accumulated enough money to guarantee a payout of $175,000 a year for the rest of your life.

What amount do I have to save to get to my goal?
The amount of savings, or "contributions," as we refer to them, depends on the three factors listed above. The younger you are, the lower the contribution. Additionally, the more you earn on your money, the lower the contribution, and of course, if you don't need much money, the lower the contribution and visa versa.

Let us look at two examples:

Example 1

Goal: To have $175,000 a year for as long as you live.

Facts: Current age 56. Retirement age is 65. Assumed interest, 6% compounded annually.

Result: If you are 56 years old, you will have to set aside into the plan $144,000 per year for ten years to reach the goal of receiving $175,000 per year or $14,583 per month per year for life staring at age 65.

Example 2

If you are 63 and want to retire at age 67 (in five years instead of ten), the contribution becomes $189,000 per year and the pension would be $103,000 per year or $8,583 per month for life. (Government rules require the actuary to reduce the pension if you fund a plan for less than ten years.)

Can't Sleep? Read On!

The retirement goal of $175,000 at age 65 has a future cash value determined by a government interest and mortality table. Based on their table, the cash amount is $1,900,000. Therefore, the future value is $1,900,000. (For my example, I have assumed interest at 6% and duration of ten years to retirement age 65.)

How much money do you have to contribute to the plan to reach your goal?

The answer is a contribution to the plan of $144,000 per year.

In future years, the contribution may increase or decrease, depending upon how much above or below the interest assumption of 6% you achieve on your investments. If you are relatively sure you will earn less than 6% on your money, the actuary can use a lower interest rate, which will cause the contributions to the plan to increase. Conversely, a higher interest rate will have the opposite effect. Contributions may also increase or decrease, depending upon changes in employee salaries. (Defined Benefit plans are usually tied to salary and years to retirement.)

> *It is important not to confuse the "pension" with the "contribution." The pension is the goal and the contribution plus expenses is the cost.*

How is the Money Invested?

The government requires that these plans to be certified by a licensed individual called an "actuary" (unless you buy the plan through an insurance company under the term "fully insured defined benefit plan," commonly known as a 412(i) plan). Instead of investing the money in stocks, bonds, real estate or any other prudent investments, all the money is invested in cash value insurance and/or annuities. The assumed earnings rate is the insurance company's guaranteed rate, usually 4%. You decide when you start a defined benefit plan if you want to be responsible for investing the money or let the insurance company do it for you.

The first thing that may come to mind is that, over time, you may be able to make more than the interest used by the plan's actuary. If you make more than what the government requires the actuary to use, the additional earnings will reduce your contributions in the future. Conversely, if you do not earn the stated interest rate, your company has to make up the difference. Trustees generally invest pension money very conservatively. (My preference, based on historical returns and moderate risk, is a portfolio comprised of 65% Stocks and 35% bonds and cash.)

What Does It Cost to Cover My Employees?

Plan design has a lot to do with what the plan costs. If you are the only participant, the cost is the contribution plus administrative compliance and actuarial fees. Adding employees increases the contribution. The actuary or consultant will illustrate what the cost is likely to be when the plan is being designed.

Generally, you should expect to receive 60% to 90% of the benefits. The older and more highly paid your employees are, the lower the percentage you will receive. Therefore, these plans work best for small employers when the work force is younger and less highly paid on average than the owners and officers. Larger companies benefit from these plans because, although the cost may initially appear high, it can be designed to benefit long-term employees more cost effectively than Profit Sharing plans.

Employee Cost Calculation

Let us take a plan that will provide a pension of 100% of salary at retirement. Your employee is age 30, earning $30,000 per year. Your contribution on her behalf is $4,000 per year. However: contributions in a defined benefit plan are not the pension; therefore *do not assume that the employee is entitled to $4,000 today.* (This concept is the hardest to understand because most people want to relate the yearly expenditure as the actual cost.)

Here is some math that shows what the cost might be:

Let us say this 30-year-old employee works for you for three years. You contributed $4,000 x 3 = $12,000. Assuming you are in the 40% plus tax bracket, your after-tax cost is $7,200. All money contributed to a pension plan is tax deductible. Think of it this way: if you took home the $12,000, you would be left with $7,200.

But we are not done.

What if the employee terminates employment after three years? How much money is she then entitled to?

The formula is derived based on the actual years worked over the total years to retirement. This is called the "accrued benefit." Based on the plan formula, the employee was scheduled to receive a pension at age 65 of $2,500 per month (100% of $30,000 a year). However, since she only worked for three years, she is entitled to 3/35th's (or .086%) of the projected pension (3/35 = 3 years of service and 35 years until retirement), which is $215 per month at age 65.

Large pension plans are often designed to pay the monthly pension for life once you reach retirement, but small companies may not be around that long, so most plans convert the pension to a current cash amount. The current cash amount is called the "present value of the accrued benefit" (PVAB).

The math: What is the PVAB of $215 per month at 5% interest due in 32 years? The answer: is $6,682.

In this example, the cost is $6,682 and not the $12,000 that you put in the plan towards her retirement. The longer an employee remains in the plan, the more closely the contribution will equal the PVAB, assuming you earned at least 5% on the money.

Vesting

But wait — there may be more savings if there is a vesting schedule. "Vesting" is the amount of the PVAB the employee is entitled to receive upon leaving the plan. If there is a typical six-year vesting schedule after three years, then the employee gets 40% of the PVAB or .40 x $6,682 = $2,673. In other words, you contributed to the plan, took a deduction for $12,000 over three years, and only paid out $2,673 when the employee left your company.

There is more. The money was at work earning at least 5% so the $12,000 grew to $13,240. $13,240 − $2,673 = $10,567. The $10,567 is called a "forfeiture" and is used to reduce future contributions or to pay administrative fees.

Thus, companies that have a fair amount of turnover plus a young employee population with an older owner will find the cost of a Defined Benefit to be lower than other types of plans.

Why Don't More Companies Have These Plans?

Large brokerage firms and insurance companies do not have the expertise to design and maintain these plans so they are not marketed like 401(k) plans. In addition, most businesses do not understand how the cost is derived so they are afraid to commit to the plan.

Things to Consider about a Defined Benefit Plan

Under this kind of plan, you have to be willing to commit to a contribution for at least five years, and understand that if you cannot live up to the commitment, the plan must be redesigned, which increases the administrative cost.

You need to appreciate that as an owner you are getting a benefit many times more valuable than a typical retirement plan. Additionally, if a larger corporation installs a Defined Benefit Plan, the cost of providing meaningful retirement benefits should be less than using a Profit Sharing Plan. The cost of operation is usually incidental to what you will receive at the end.

The only people not satisfied with Defined Benefit plans are those who stop them almost as soon as they establish them or because the cost becomes too onerous. Then again, that is part of plan design. If you know you will stop the plan in a short amount of time or want to reduce the cost, this information will help the actuary design the plan to give you the proper outcome.

How Do Employees Relate to the Plan?

Young, short-service employees do not find much value in a benefit that is promised when they retire. For these employees, we recommend a 401(k) Plan. However, your key employees will find the Defined Benefit Plan extremely valuable. You are promising them a guaranteed pension if they stay with you. Surveys have shown that if an employee has his retirement income taken care of, he will be a more productive employee.

What Else Do I Need to Know?

Plans should be designed to meet your goals. If you are a small employer, design the plan to benefit you as much as possible (in most cases, 60% to 80% of the contribution can go to the owner). For larger plans, consider a budget and design the plan accordingly. For example, if the industry standard is 50% of salary as a pension at retirement but, based on your budget, you can only do 30%, simply design it that way. The actuary will do cost-to-benefit studies for you.

An Enrolled Actuary certifies the plan and assists with design, and the plan is reviewed yearly to be sure you are on schedule. Changes to increase or decrease the benefits or contributions can be made along the way. This is an important feature to Defined Benefit Plans. If your business is not making money, the benefits can be cut back. Conversely, if you need more tax deductions, the plan benefit can be increased.

Adjustments are also made annually for changes in employees, salaries and plan earnings. Your TPA or actuary will prepare all necessary government filings and arrange to pay benefits for those employees who terminate during the year.

Is a Defined Benefit Pension Plan is Right for My Company?

Retirement plans are based on age, salary and years of employment. If you provide your TPA or Actuary with a list of all employees with their date of hire, date of birth and W-2 wages, they can do a study. There is a cost to do these studies, but most TPA's will give you some credit toward the installation of the plan if you decide to go forward.

Summary

1 Defined Benefit Plans provide a monthly stream of payments you can't outlive.
2 You can buy a pension of 100% of salary up to the government's limit.
3 A 401(k) or Profit Sharing Plan is dependent on how much you save and earn on investments.
4 The Trustee hires an investment manager to invest assets on behalf of the plan.
5 Small employers with a few employees can save more money through Defined

Benefit Plans than through other retirement savings plans.

6 Employers often overlook these plans either because they lack understanding or because they think the plan is not affordable.

17

Roles and Responsibilities

WHEN AN EMPLOYER RETAINS A TPA TO PROVIDE ADMINISTRATIVE COMPLI-
ANCE AND RECORDKEEPING SERVICES, IT IS IMPORTANT THAT THE EMPLOYER
CLEARLY UNDERSTAND THE ROLE THE TPA WILL PLAY. The following discussion
identifies the tasks necessary to operate a retirement plan.

Plan Installation

Party Responsible – TPA:
1 Assists employer with a plan document and Summary Plan Description
  (SPD) based on the employer's plan design information. May refer employer
  to an ERISA attorney.
2 Explains the blackout period necessary to convert "pooled accounts" to "share
  accounts," or to reconcile information received from a past service provider.

3 Coordinates with record keeper to allow for participant access to their voice response system and Internet site at the completion of the plan installation.
4 Prepares all paperwork required to submit the plan to the IRS for a Determination Letter.

Party Responsible – Employer:
5 Provides accurate and clear plan design criteria to provider.
6 Sets forth all benefits, rights and features of the pre-existing plan, (if applicable).
7 Provides complete and accurate employee census information, when requested.
8 Obtains advice on any legal and tax ramifications affecting the plan.
9 Obtains a surety bond, as required by ERISA.
10 Notifies TPA of any other retirement plans, terminated or maintained, by the employer.
11 Distributes the SPD's and investment information to all eligible employees.
12 Explains plan provisions and operations to all eligible employees.
13 Assists employees in completing forms or documents.
14 Provides enrollment and election information to record keeper.

Standard Administration Services

Party Responsible – TPA:
15 Coordinates procedures with investment provider.
16 Verifies benefit payments, participant terminations, hardships or loans, and required minimum distributions in accordance with the employer's or participant's instructions.
17 Maintains participant records for vesting and forfeitures.
18 Prepares annual compliance reports for the employer.

Party Responsible – Employer:
19 Provides complete, accurate and timely information and approvals in the manner and within the time frames reasonably requested by the TPA.
20 Determines employee eligibility according to the plan rules.
21 Notifies newly eligible employees of their right to participate in the Plan.
22 Provides accurate payroll data and issues checks promptly following the close of

each payroll period, but no later than 15 business days after each month end.

23 Makes sure provider issues quarterly benefit statements to each participant.

24 Verifies benefit claims, such as Domestic Relations Orders (QRDO's), loan requests, and hardships.

25 Promptly reviews for accuracy and completeness all plan reports or confirmations.

Compliance Testing

Party Responsible – TPA:

26 Performs actual deferral percentage (ADP) test (IRC Sec. 401(k)(3)) annually.

27 Performs actual contribution percentage (ACP) (IRC Sec. 401(m)) annually.

28 Performs minimum coverage test (IRC Sec. 410(b)(1)(A) and (B)) annually.

29 Performs top-heavy test (IRC Sec. 416) annually.

30 Performs elective deferrals test (IRC Sec. 402(g) and Sec. 401(a)(3)) annually.

31 Performs annual additions test under IRC Sec. 415(c) annually.

32 Calculates excess distributions necessary to correct the Plan's testing failures.

Party Responsible – Employer:

33 Transmits plan data to TPA for nondiscrimination testing and reporting when applicable.

34 Authorizes actions and remit any payments to satisfy the nondiscrimination tests.

Reporting and Withholding

Party Responsible – TPA:

35 Prepares signature-ready IRS Form 5500 and related schedules.

36 IRS Form 1099-R to be completed by the trust company or investment provider.

Party Responsible – Employer:

37 Supplies TPA with the information necessary to prepare Form 5500 and related schedules.

38 Reviews and files IRS Form 5500 and related schedules by the due date.

39 Provides trust company or investment provider with necessary information concerning Form 1099-R income tax withholding when applicable.

Additional Services

There may be a need for additional services because of specific planning needs. The following services are generally billed separately by the TPA.

Employee Payroll Deferrals
Manual payroll processing or payroll compilation from different sources.

Consulting Services
Technical consulting for legal or actuarial issues;
Additional discrimination testing;
Investment accounting/reconciliation;
Audit assistance; and
IRS determination letter submission.

Multiple Eligibility Requirements
The Plan may have one eligibility period for the employee deferrals another for matching and another for the profit sharing plan.

Communications
Customized or additional reports, letters or lost participant communications.

Outside Assets
Account for assets not accounted for by record keeper, such as company stock.

Plan Termination
Provide all government filings, reports, participant disclosures, and distributions with participant-level tax reporting. Follow through with all participant and governmental issues until all assets are distributed.

1

Recurring Deadlines for 401(k) Plans

MOST EMPLOYERS ASSUME THAT THE PEOPLE THEY HIRE TO MANAGE THE PLAN ARE TAKING CARE OF GOVERNMENT REPORTING, COMPLIANCE TESTING AND PARTICIPANT DISCLOSURES. In fact, most service agreements state that you are hiring the providers to assist you with these mandatory requirements. This means that you may have to provide them with information so they can assist you with these requirements.

One of the biggest complaints employers bring against providers is incomplete forms and late discrimination tests. Often it is a lack of urgency on behalf of the employer and a lack of clarity on behalf of the provider that creates missing data and delays. (Remember my statements about lack of coordination between company officers, your in-house administrator and the service provider.) No matter whom you hire to manage the plan do not assume everything is going to be done for you.

Here is a calendar of yearly deadlines you should be mindful of.

Deadlines — Calendar Year Plan	
Jan 31	**Distribution Reporting to Participant**
	Form	1099-R
	Due Date	Jan 31
	Responsible Party	Payer

Jan 31 or Feb 10	**Annual Return of Withheld Federal Income Tax**
	Form	945
	Due Date	1/31 or 2/10 if taxes timely paid
	Responsible Party	Payer

Feb 28	**Distribution Reporting to IRS**	
	Form	1096 transmittal with Forms 1099-R
	Due Date	Feb 28
	Responsible Party	Payer

Mar 15	**Corrective Distribution for Failed ADP/ACP Without 10% Excise Tax & Filing of Corporate Tax Return and Plan Sponsor Contribution due**	
	Due Date	Correction by 2 ½ months after plan year end
	Responsible Party	Employer/Trustee

Mar 15	**Deadline for Deductibility** (without extension, see below)	
	Form	1120

	Deadlines — Calendar Year Plan (continued)	
	Due Date	2 1/2 months after fiscal year end
	Responsible Party	Corporate Employer

	Summary Plan Description (for January 1 entry)	
	Due Date	Within 90 days of becoming a participant
	Responsible Party	Plan Administrator

	Excise Taxes (on ADP/ACP test corrections 2 1/2 months after plan year end)	
	Form	5330
	Due Date	Last day of the 15th month after the plan year end to which the contribution or excess aggregate contributions relate
	Responsible Party	Plan Sponsor

Apr 15	**Distribution of 402(g) (Excess Deferrals)**	
	Due Date	Apr 15
	Responsible Party	Plan Administrator/Trustee

	Filing of Individual and/or Partnership Tax Returns & Contribution Deadlines for Deductibility for Unincorporated Entities without extension	
	Form	1040, 1065 with Schedule K-1
	Due Date	15th day of 4th month after end of partnership (or personal) tax year
	Responsible Party	Sole Proprietor or Partnership

Deadlines — Calendar Year Plan (continued)

Jul 28	**Summary of Material Modifications**	
	Due Date	210th day after end of plan year when modification was adopted
	Responsible Party	Plan Administrator

Jul 31	**Excise Taxes (on prohibited transactions)**	
	Form	5330, Part III
	Due Date	Last day of 7th month after end of tax year of disqualified person
	Responsible Party	Disqualified person involved in prohibited transaction

	Annual Report of Plan (with Schedules)	
	Form	5500 series filing
	Due Date	Last day of 7th month beginning after end of plan year (or as extended)
	Responsible Party	Plan Sponsor

	Request for Extension to File 5500 Series	
	Form	5558
	Due Date	Last day of 7th month beginning after end of plan year
	Responsible Party	Plan Sponsor

	Request for Automatic Extension–5500 Series (2½ months)	
	Form	5558
	Due Date	Due Date for Form 5500
	Responsible Party	Plan Sponsor

Deadlines — Calendar Year Plan (continued)

	Statement of Deferred Benefits	
	Due Date	No later than filing of Form 5500 (Schedule SSA)
	Responsible Party	Plan Administrator

Aug 15	Extended Deadline for Filing of Individual Tax Returns (and Contribution Deadline for Deductibility)	
	Form	1040
	Due Date	4 months after original filing deadline
	Responsible Party	Sole Proprietor/Partner

Sep 30	Summary Annual Report	
	Due Date	Last day of 9th month beginning after end of plan year (or as extended)
	Responsible Party	Plan Administrator

Oct 15	Extended Deadline for filing of Form 5500	
	Form	5500
	Due Date	2 1/2 months after original filing deadline
	Responsible Party	Plan Sponsor

Deadlines — Calendar Year Plan (continued)

	Extended Deadline for filing of Individual Tax Return (and final contribution deadline for Deductibility for Unincorporated Entities)	
	Form	1040, From 1065 with Schedule K-1
	Due Date	6 months after original due date
	Responsible Party	Sole Proprietor or Partner and Partnership

	Safe Harbor Plan Notice (and Contingent Notice for 3% safe harbor contribution, if applicable)	
Dec 1	Due Date	30-90 days prior to start of plan year using Safe Harbor design
	Responsible Party	Plan Administrator or Plan Sponsor

	Supplemental Notice for Safe Harbor Plan that issued Contingent Notice at beginning of year as to whether 3% Safe Harbor will be made for the current year	
	Due Date	At least 30 days before end of plan year
	Responsible Party	Plan Administrator

	Prospective Amendment to Remove Safe Harbor Status for Following Year	
Dec 31	Due Date	No later than December 31 of current year
	Responsible Party	Plan Sponsor / Plan Administrator

Deadlines — Calendar Year Plan (continued)

	Corrective Distribution for Failed ADP/ACP with 10% Excise Tax or QNEC Distribution	
	Due Date	Last day of plan year following the year of failure
	Responsible Party	Plan Sponsor / Plan Administrator

	Self correction of significant qualification failures (Rev. Proc. 2003-44)	
	Due Date	Last day of second plan year following the year of failure last day of third plan year after ADP/ACP failure
	Responsible Party	Plan Sponsor / Plan Administrator

Plan Fiduciary Checklist

Plan Document and Design

1 Does your plan have an IRS-approved document in place and is the document up-to-date for recent law changes?
2 Has your plan been designed with the assistance of a competent professional so it is designed to meet the needs of the company?
3 Does your plan have an up-to-date summary plan description (SPD) and have you distributed the SPD to participants when required?
4 If you have any workers (including independent contractors or temporary employees) at your company who are not covered under the plan, does your plan document specifically exclude them from participation?
5 If you, your family or your company have ownership rights (controlled group)

in any other businesses, have you received advice concerning the possible consequences to your plan?

Plan Fiduciaries

6 Are the plan fiduciaries (e.g., plan committee, trustees, officers and owners) aware they are fiduciaries? Have they been informed of their responsibilities under ERISA?

7 Are plan investment fiduciaries appointed in accordance with the plan and trust documents?

8 Do the plan committee and other fiduciaries meet at least annually?

9 Is a due diligence file maintained with the notes, minutes, agenda, background information and supporting documentation for plan and investment decisions made at the fiduciary meetings?

10 Do the plan fiduciaries ensure that the plan collects and invests the employee deferrals in as timely a manner as possible?

11 Is your plan covered by a fidelity bond of at least 10% of plan assets (up to $500,000) and does the bond cover plan fiduciaries as well as other employees or third parties that handle or have access to plan assets?

Plan Investments

12 Does your plan have a written investment policy statement?

13 Does your plan have investments in at least the following investment categories so that participants may invest in a "broad range" of funds?

a Stable value investment, guaranteed investment contract (GIC) or money market fund?

b U.S. government or corporate bonds;

c Large-cap U.S. equities;

d Mid-small cap U.S. equities;

e International or global equities

14 Have the plan fiduciaries reviewed the plan's investments in the last 12 months? Was each investment compared to its peer group and the appropriate index for performance over periods of 1, 3, 5, and 10 years?

15 Was the review conducted in accordance with the investment policy statement?

16 In order to properly review the investment, did your investment provider

give you information on the proper peer group and indices, historical performance, expenses, volatility and other significant factors? If not, did you accumulate that information for review?

17 Was the review documented in plan fiduciary/investment committee due diligence file, including the materials reviewed by the committee and any other notes or analysis used to determine whether to retain, add or remove investment options?

18 Are investment costs reasonable in comparison to the appropriate benchmarks? Do you fully understand all investment costs and the services that are provided for these costs?

19 Have you removed an investment from your plan, or placed it on "watch," because of its underperformance or other failure to satisfy the investment policy statement or ERISA's requirements?

20 Does your plan avoid overlap of similar stock holding among investment options by offering options from more than one investment management company?

21 Are you limited in your ability to select superior funds because your investment provider limits the number of funds from other providers?

22 Does your plan provide employee enrollment programs explaining the importance of participation in the plan, saving for retirement, and investment basics?

23 Does your plan provide ongoing employee investment education materials and/or programs?

24 Does your plan provide lifestyle funds or asset allocation models for employees who lack the investment knowledge to evaluate and select individual investment options and allocate their accounts among them?

ERISA Section 404(c) Requirements

25 If your plan intends to obtain the fiduciary protections available under ERISA Section 404(c), does the SPD or a written notice to participants provide the following notification:

a Participants will be able to direct their investments;

b The plan intends to comply with 404(c) and plan fiduciaries may be relieved of liability for losses; and

c The name, address and phone number of the 404(c) plan fiduciary responsible for providing information upon request and for receiving and complying with participant investment instructions

26 Have all participants received information about each of the options available under the plan?

27 Have all participants received or had access to information regarding investment concepts (including explanation of the types of investments, risk/return applicable to each, impact of time horizon on investment decisions, etc.) in the last 12 months?

28 Does the Form 5500 indicate that your plan intends to comply with ERISA 404(c) requirements?

Note: Not every item on this checklist is a legal requirement, but if you are not complying with a majority of these items, you are increasing your fiduciary liability.

Investment Policy Statement[*]

THE INVESTMENT POLICY STATEMENT (IPS) IS A DOCUMENT THAT ESTABLISHES THE INVESTMENT PROCEDURE FOR THE PLAN AND SETS FORTH GUIDELINES FOR SELECTION OF PLAN INVESTMENTS. It goes on to state that the Plan will abide by regulation 404(c) and offer a selection of mutual funds that satisfies a broad range of fund styles. It will also offer guidance on when to make changes and the criteria to use to make these changes.

The IPS is to investments what the administration guide or the Roles and Responsibility statement is to day-to-day administration of the Plan.

Curiously enough, there is no requirement that a Plan have an Investment Policy Statement or, for that matter, an administration manual. Once you put retirement plan procedures in writing, you are holding yourself to a hirer standard. If you follow the document, you can hold all involved accountable for their

---

[*] Parts of this IPS were provided by Nationwide Financial.

actions, assuming you have shared these documents with all charged with the responsibility to manage the plan. This is advisable if the business owner is not involved in day-to-day decision making about the Plan.

The following is a sample of an Investment Policy Statement.

I Overview and Purpose

A Overview of Investment Policy

The ABC Company 401(k) Plan is a retirement plan established by ABC Company ("Plan Sponsor") for the benefit of the participating employees and their beneficiaries. The Plan is qualified under Section 401(a) of the Internal Revenue Code ("IRC") and is a 401(k) plan that permits voluntary pre-tax deferrals by participants from their pay.

The Plan permits participants to direct the investment of their accounts.

Employer-matching contributions may be made at the Plan Sponsor's discretion.

Eligible employees are responsible for determining how much to contribute as a deferral of their pay, up to the allowable limit each year, and allocating their monies among the investment alternatives offered by the Plan.

The ultimate authority to establish the investment structure, to prepare and amend this Investment Policy Statement and to select and review the investment alternatives resides with the Plan Sponsor.

B Purpose of Investment Policy

The purpose of this Investment Policy Statement ("IPS") is to establish the investment structure for the Plan and to adopt a set of guidelines for the selection of the Plan's investment alternatives and for the periodic evaluation, or monitoring, of the investment alternatives.

This IPS is intended to be consistent with the criteria for an ERISA Section 404(c) Plan. To comply with ERISA Section 404(c), the Plan must satisfy the conditions in the regulations. This includes designating a broad range of investment alternatives that permit participants to make choices regarding the manner in which the assets in their individual accounts are invested. It should also afford the participants the opportunity to materially affect the potential returns on their accounts and the degree of risk involved.

C **Investment Advisor or Broker**

The Plan Sponsor will engage an advisor familiar with both investing for retirement and the law associated with retirement plans called ERISA to help administer this investment policy. The advisor will from time to time present alternatives to the current investment structure to ascertain that the current investment provider is accomplishing the goals of the plan.

II Investments

A **Investment Portfolios**

The Plan will allow participants to create investment portfolios by allocating their accounts among a group of investment alternatives that constitute a broad range of asset classes and investment styles. From time to time, the Employer or Investment Committee will review the Plan's investment structure.

In addition, the Plan will include asset allocation funds, which will enable participants to direct the investment of their accounts into a managed portfolio designed to be consistent with their time horizons and risk tolerances.

B **Broad Range of Funds**

In order to offer a broad range of investment alternatives so that each participant and beneficiary has a reasonable opportunity to

1 Materially affect both the potential return and degree of risk relating to his or her accounts,

2 Choose from diversified investment alternatives, and

3 Diversify his or her investment to minimize the risk of large losses.

The Plan will offer a selection of mutual funds. In the process of selecting the funds to be used as the Plan's investment choices, the Employer or Investment Committee will first select the asset classes and investment styles intended to satisfy the broad range requirement. The Morningstar style box will be used as the criteria. The broad range of funds will include Large, Medium and Small Cap funds in the Growth, Blend and Value categories. This will be called the Core Selection. At a minimum, the Plan's investments should provide participants the opportunity to invest in funds designed to have a stable value fund, such as a Money Market Fund, a bond fund and an equity fund.

C **Additional Funds**

The Employer or Investment Committee may also decide to offer funds in addition to the Core Selection. These funds may include funds that take greater than normal risk. These funds may be added to provide additional investment alternatives.

In selecting these additional Funds, the Employer or Investment Committee will consider factors such as the sophistication of their employees, investment education, communication and advice programs.

D **Asset Allocation Models**

The plan will provide participants with general financial and investment information. This will include asset allocation models to assist them in making their allocation decisions. Participants will be provided with a questionnaire that measures their individual risk tolerance and investment time horizon and may select a model portfolio based on the results of that questionnaire.

E **Asset Allocation Funds**

To enable participants to benefit from the asset allocation expertise of investment professionals, the Plan will provide participants with five asset allocation funds.

- *Conservative*: This fund seeks to maximize total investment return through income, and, secondarily, through long-term growth of capital.
- *Moderately Conservative*: The fund seeks to maximize total investment return through income and secondarily through long-term growth of capital.
- *Moderate*: This fund seeks to maximize total investment return through growth of capital and income.
- *Moderately Aggressive*: This fund seeks to maximize total investment return primarily through growth of capital, but also through income.
- *Aggressive*: This fund seeks to maximize total investment return through growth of capital.

The purpose of the asset allocation funds is to provide participants with investment options professionally designed to take into account risk tolerances and investment time horizons. Additionally, the asset allocation funds will automatically be re-balanced periodically to maintain the strategic asset allocation.

III Portfolio Standards

The Employer or Investment Committee will follow a process to prudently select, monitor and, when appropriate, remove Funds. The Funds will be selected from among a universe of funds so that there is reasonable assurance that an adequate number of funds have been reviewed and that the Funds are representative of superior investment alternatives available to the Plan.

The following are the guidelines for the selection, monitoring, retention and removal of Funds.

A Selection of Funds

1 **Evaluation Guidelines**. The Employer or Investment Committee will create a peer group of funds for each targeted asset class consisting of funds then screen the universe of funds based on the following evaluation guidelines:

a **Sharpe Ratio**. The investment performance of the funds, relative to the risk taken by the managers, will be evaluated.

b **Trailing performance**. The investment performance of the funds will be evaluated using weighted trailing annualized total returns.

c **Rolling Information Ratio**. The consistency of risk-adjusted investment performance of the funds, relative to their benchmarks, will be evaluated.

d **Rolling Performance Consistency**. The total returns of the funds will be evaluated using rolling periods to minimize the end period dominance of recent performance history and to provide more comprehensive performance data to evaluate.

e **Rolling Selection Return**. Each fund's returns will be compared to the market benchmarks of various investment styles to determine the custom portfolio benchmark that best explains the pattern and consistency of each Fund's returns. The Employer or Investment Committee will then compare each fund's performance to its custom portfolio benchmark to determine the value added or subtracted by its manager.

2 **Additional Fund Analysis**. As a secondary screening process in selecting a fund, the Employer or Investment Committee will also evaluate additional factors as follows:

a High operating expenses

b High individual holding concentration

c High economic sector concentration
d High performance volatility
e High portfolio turnover
f Low style purity
g High duration bet
h Low credit quality average
i Low manager tenure
j Low asset base

3 **Fund selection**. For each peer group, the Employer or Investment Committee will review three funds which best satisfy the evaluation guidelines. The Employer or Investment Committee will then select one or more Funds for the Plan participants to provide a broad range of investment alternatives.

B **Investment of Accounts without Participant Direction**

If a participant fails to provide the Plan with an investment direction, the Employer or Investment Committee will direct the investment of the participant's account, until the participant provides direction. Each non-directed participant's money will be invested in the moderate asset allocation portfolio, or another balanced fund, until the Employer or Investment Committee decides to change this decision for all participants who have not provided investment directions or until the Employer or Investment Committee determines that a different investment selection is appropriate for a participant. In making these decisions, the Employer or Investment Committee is not responsible for inquiring into the specific goals or needs of a participant.

Glossary of Terms

—A—

Accrued Benefit

The amount of pension earned to date. For example, if the projected pension at age 65 is $2000 a month and the participant is 45 years old, at age 55 he will have an accrued benefit of $1000. This example is based on the "fractional method." This means the participant accrues 1/20th of $2000 each year, if he has 20 years to reach his normal retirement date.

Accrued Interest

The amount credited to a bond or other fixed-income security between the last payment and when the security is sold.

Active Participant

In a 401(k) plan an employee is considered an "active participant" if he or she makes a deferral. In a profit sharing plan, you become an "active participant" if any money is allocated to your account because you met eligibility.

Actual Contribution Test (ACP)
The non-discrimination test for matching contributions in a 401(k) plan.

Actual Deferral Percentage Test (ADP) (Also known as the "ADP Test.")
This is the non-discrimination test for participant salary deferrals in a 401(k) plan.

Annuity
A contract that you enter in with an insurance company that agrees to make regular payments to individual(s) for life or for a fixed period.

Appreciation
The increase in the value of an investment.

Asset Allocation
Dividing your investment portfolio among the major asset classes.

Asset Allocation Fund
A portfolio that spreads its investments among a wide variety of mutual funds.

Asset
Property that has economic value (such as cash, stocks, bonds and real estate).

— B —

Balanced Fund
A mutual fund or collective trust that maintains a balanced portfolio, which generally means 40% bonds and 60% stocks.

Beta
A measure of a stock's risk relative to the market, usually the Standard &

Poor's 500 index. The market's beta is always 1.0. A beta higher than 1.0 indicates that, on average, when the market rises, the mutual fund or stock will rise to a greater extent and likewise when the market falls. A beta lower than 1.0 indicates that, on average, the stock will move to a lesser extent than the market. The higher the beta the greater the risk.

Bond

A certificate of debt issued by a corporation or the government. Bonds generally pay a specific rate of interest and pay back the original investment after a specified period of time.

Book Value Per Share

The accounting value of a share of common stock. It is determined by dividing the net worth of the company (common stock plus retained earnings) by the number of shares outstanding.

Buy-and-Hold

A strategy in which the stock portion of your portfolio is fully invested in the stock market at all times.

— C —

Capital Gain

An increase in the value of a capital asset such as common stock. If the asset is sold, the gain is a "realized" capital gain. A capital gain may be short-term (one year or less) or long-term (more than one year).

Certificate of Deposit

A bank deposit that pays a specified rate of interest for a certain period of time.

Commission

Broker's fee for buying or selling securities.

Common Stock

An investment representing ownership interest in a corporation.

Compliance Testing
Testing required by the IRS to make sure that the 401(k) plan is fair to both highly compensated and non-highly compensated employees.

Compounding
The ability of an asset to generate earnings that are reinvested and which generate their own earnings (earnings on earnings).

Contribution
A payment, deposit or premium made to a retirement plan such as a 401(k), profit sharing or defined benefit pension plan.

Custodian
The bank or trust company that maintains a retirement plan's assets, including its portfolio of securities or some record of them. Provides safekeeping of securities but has no role in portfolio management.

Cyclical Industry
An industry, such as automobiles, whose performance is closely tied to the condition of the general economy. The company (and their stock) do well during good economic times and not as well during poor economic times.

— D —

Defined Benefit Pension Plan
A defined benefit plan is an employer-maintained plan that pays out a specific, pre-determined amount to retirees.

Defined Contribution Plan
A defined contribution plan does not promise a specific benefit at retirement but allows discretionary contributions to a plan's investment fund.

Deflation
The increase of purchasing power due to a general decrease in the prices of goods and services.

Depreciation

Decrease in the value of an investment over time.

Discount bond

A bond that is valued at less than its face amount.

Discount broker

A stockbroker who charges a reduced commission and provides no investment advice.

Discount Rate

The interest rate used in discounting future cash flows; also called the "capitalization rate."

Distributions and Withdrawals

When money is withdrawn from a retirement plan, the withdrawal is referred to as a "distribution." Retirement plan assets can be withdrawn without penalty after age 59 1/2. Employees are required to begin taking distributions after age 70 1/2.

Diversification

The practice of spreading risk by investing in a number of securities that have different return patterns over time.

Dividend

Payments by a company to its stockholders. A dividend is usually a portion of profits.

Dividend Yield

Annual dividends per share divided by price per share. An indication of the income generated by a share of stock. The dividend yield plus capital gains percentage equals total return.

Dollar-Cost Averaging

A process of buying securities at regular intervals and at a fixed dollar amount. When prices are lower, the investor buys more shares or units; when prices are higher, the investor purchases fewer shares or units. Over time, this typically results in a better average price for all shares or units purchased.

Dow Jones Industrial Average (DJIA)
Price-weighted average of 30 actively traded blue-chip stocks.

— E —

Earnings Per Share
The net income of the firm divided by the number of common stock shares outstanding.

Earnings Yield
Earnings per share for the most recent 12 months divided by market price per share. Relates the generation of earnings to share price. (It is the inverse of the price-earnings ratio.)

EGTRRA
The Economic Growth and Tax Reconciliation Act of 2001

Eligibility
A participant becomes eligible for the plan upon meeting requirements (such as minimum age 21 and one year of service with the employer). The plan document spells out the eligibility rules.

Employer Matching Contribution
Money the employer contributes to the employee's 401(k) account, generally based upon the amount invested by the employee. For example, 50 cents for every dollar invested by the employee.

Equities
Investments in which the investors obtain a portion of ownership. Real estate and common stocks represent equity instruments. Usually, their chief benefit is potential growth in value. (Also another word for "stock.")

ERISA

The Employee Retirement Income Security Act of 1974, known as ERISA, a comprehensive law dealing with all areas of pensions and employee benefits and pension plans. ERISA includes requirements on pension disclosure, participation standards, vesting rules, funding, and administration.

ERISA protects plan assets by requiring that those persons or entities who exercise discretionary control or authority over plan management or plan assets, or have discretionary authority or responsibility for the administration of a plan, or provide investment advice to a plan for compensation or have any authority or responsibility to do so are subject to fiduciary responsibilities. Plan fiduciaries include, for example, plan trustees, plan administrators, and members of a plan's investment committee.

The primary responsibility of fiduciaries is to run the plan solely in the interest of participants and beneficiaries and for the exclusive purpose of providing benefits and paying plan expenses. Fiduciaries must act prudently and must diversify the plan's investments in order to minimize the risk of large losses. In addition, they must follow the terms of plan documents to the extent that the plan terms are consistent with ERISA. They also must avoid conflicts of interest. In other words, they may not engage in transactions on behalf of the plan that benefit parties related to the plan, such as other fiduciaries, services providers, or the plan sponsor.

Fiduciaries that do not follow these principles of conduct may be personally liable to restore any losses to the plan, or to restore any profits made through improper use of plan assets. Courts may take whatever action is appropriate against fiduciaries that breach their duties under ERISA including their removal.

ESOP

Employee stock ownership plan, or "ESOP," is a defined contribution plan similar in operation to a profit sharing plan that is intended to invest in the sponsoring company's stock.

Exchange Traded Funds (ETF)

A security that tracks an index, a commodity or a grouping of assets. ETFs trade like a stock on a stock exchange. (While Mutual funds are priced once a day, an ETF experiences price changes throughout the day, just like a stock.)

Expense Ratio

The ratio of total expenses to net assets of a mutual fund. (Expenses include management fees, 12(b)1 charges, if any, the cost of shareholder mailings and other administrative expenses. The ratio is listed in a fund's prospectus.)

— F —

Fiduciary

A person is a retirement plan fiduciary if such person does any of the following:

1 Exercises any discretionary authority or control over the management or dis-position of the plan assets.
2 Renders investment advice for a fee or other compensation or has any author-ity or responsibility over plan assets.
3 Has any discretionary authority or responsibility in the administration of the plan.

Additionally, an individual or a trust institution charged with the duty of acting for the benefit of another party as to matters coming within the scope of the relationship between them. The relationship between a guardian and his ward, an agent and his principal, an attorney and his client, one partner and another partner, a trustee and a beneficiary, each is an example of fidu-ciary relationship.

Fidelity Bond

ERISA requires fiduciaries and every person who handles plan funds to be covered by a fidelity bond. The fidelity bond protects the plan against fraudu-lent or dishonest acts by those covered by the bond. The bond must cover at least 10 percent of the total plan assets during the plan year. The minimum bond is $1000 and the maximum bond is $500,000.

Fiscal Year

An accounting period consisting of 12 consecutive months.

Fixed-Income Securities

Investments that represent an IOU from the government or a corporation to the investor and offer specific payments at predetermined times. Public and private bonds, government securities, and the 401(k)'s guaranteed accounts, are fixed-income investments. Guaranteed fixed-income accounts offer investors a guarantee against the loss of both principal and the interest earned on that principal.

Form 5500

The annual report/return filing required by the federal government on behalf of a qualified retirement plan.

401(k) Plan

A tax-deferred retirement plan that can be offered by businesses of any kind. A company's 401(k) plan can have several accounts. Money can be contributed by the employee only. Money can also be contributed by the employer by means of matching or profit sharing. A 401(k) plan carries many unique advantages for both employer and employee.

403(b) Plan

Section 403(b) of the Internal Revenue Code allows employees of public school systems and certain charitable and nonprofit organizations to establish tax-deferred retirement plans which can be funded with mutual funds or annuities. This similar to a 401(k) plan.

Fully Insured Plan

A Defined Benefit Pension Plan known as a 412(i) plan. A 412(i) Plan must invest exclusively in annuity and life insurance contracts.

— G —

Guaranteed Investment (Interest) Contract (GIC)

A debt instrument sold by Insurance Companies and often bought for retirement plans. The word "guaranteed" refers to the interest rate paid on the GIC. (The company issuing the GIC makes the guarantee, not the U.S. Government.)

— H —

HCE

A highly compensated employee. An employee is considered to be a highly compensated employee if he meets a certain salary threshold or owns more than 5% of the company anytime during the current year or the preceding year. Lineal descendants and lineal ascendants are also considered a HCE.

— I —

Income Fund

A common trust fund or mutual fund that primarily seeks current income rather than growth of capital. It will tend to invest in stocks and bonds that normally pay high dividends and interest.

Index Fund

A common trust fund or mutual fund that seeks to mirror general stock-market performance by matching its portfolio to a broad-based index, most often the Standard & Poor's 500-stock index.

Individual Retirement Account (IRA) Regular

A personal, tax-sheltered retirement account available to wage earners not covered by a company retirement plan or, if covered, meeting certain income limitations.

Individual Retirement Account (IRA) Rollover

A provision in the IRA law allowing individuals who receive lump-sum payments from pension or profit-sharing plans to "roll over" into, or invest that sum in, an IRA. IRA funds can be "rolled over" from one investment to another.

Index

A statistical measure of the changes in a portfolio representing a market. The Standard & Poor's 500 is the most well-known index. It measures the overall change in the value of the 500 stocks of the largest firms in the U.S.

Inflation
The loss of purchasing power due to a general rise in the prices of goods and services.

Insider Trading
Trading by management or others who have special access to unpublished information.

Integration
A pension design tool in which contributions reflect the existence of Social Security benefits. In this process, FICA taxes are considered part of the contribution to the pension fund. Since Social Security provides a greater percentage benefit to lower paid employees, integration allows the company to increase contributions to higher paid employees.

Interest
What a borrower pays a lender for the use of money. This is the income you receive from a bond, note, certificate of deposit, or other form of IOU.

Investment Adviser
A person who manages assets and creates investment portfolios for a fee or a percentage of assets invested.

IRA
Individual Retirement Account, a retirement plan that offers tax deductible contributions and tax deferred growth.

IRC Internal Revenue Code
The text containing the rules pertaining to the taxation system in the United States.

IRS
The Internal Revenue Service, the governmental agency responsible for collecting taxes and enforcing the Internal Revenue Code.

—J—

Junk bond

A bond purchased for speculative purposes. They are usually rated BB and lower, and they have a higher default risk.

—K—

Key Employee

An employee meeting one of three criteria

1 A more than 5% owner; or
2 A more than 1% owner whose compensation is greater than $150,000: or
3 An officer who has compensation of $135,000 or more (subject to cost of living adjustments)

—L—

Lagging indicator

Economic indicator that changes directions *after* business conditions have turned around.

Late Trading

The buying and selling of funds at a particular day's price after the close of the markets. Generally takes advantage of international stocks due to the different time zones of overseas markets.

Leading indicator

Economic indicator that changes direction *in advance of* general business conditions.

Limit Order

An order placed with a broker to buy or sell at a price as good or better than the specified limit price.

Liquidity

The degree of ease and certainty of value with which a security can be converted into cash.

— M —

Margin
   The use of borrowed money to purchase securities (buying "on margin").

Market Capitalization
   Number of common stock shares outstanding times share price. Provides a measure of a corporation's market value.

Market Order
   An order placed with a broker to buy or sell a security at whatever the price may be when the order is executed.

Market Risk
   The volatility of a stock price relative to the overall market or index as indicated by beta. (See definition of "beta" in the Glossary above).

Market Timing
   The rapid in-and-out trading enabling one to leave the market entirely during downturns and reinvesting when it heads back up.

Maturity
   The length of time until the principal amount of a bond must be repaid.

Money Market Fund
   A common trust fund or mutual fund that aims to pay money market interest rates. This is accomplished by investing in safe, highly liquid securities, including bank certificates of deposit, commercial paper, U.S. government securities and repurchase agreements. Money funds make these high interest securities available to the average investor seeking immediate income and high investment safety.

Mutual Fund
   An open-end investment company that buys back or redeems its shares at

current net asset value. Most mutual funds continuously offer new shares to investors. The management of a fund buys securities to diversify the portfolio and minimize risk of large losses.

— N —

Named Fiduciary

The person(s) or entity responsible for the Plan. The purpose of a named fiduciary is to identify to participants and the government who is responsible for the plan.

NASDAQ

The National Association of Securities Dealers Automated Quotations System. This is a computerized system that provides up-to-the-minute price quotations on about 5,000 of the more actively traded over-the-counter stocks.

Net Asset Value (NAV)

The current market worth of a mutual fund share. It is calculated daily by taking the fund's total assets, securities, cash and any accrued earnings, deducting liabilities, and dividing the remainder by the number of shares outstanding.

Nonqualified Plan

A pension plan that does not meet the requirements for preferential tax treatment. This type of plan allows an employer more flexibility and freedom with coverage requirements, benefit structures, and financing methods.

— O —

Overbought

A security (usually a stock) that has had a sharp rise, usually as a result vigorous buying, making prices too high. This is the opposite of being "oversold." (See below.)

Oversold

A security (usually a stock, but also sometimes a whole market) believed to have declined to an unreasonable level due to vigorous selling. This is the opposite of being "overbought." (See above.)

Over-the-Counter Market

A communications network through which trades of bonds, non-listed stocks, and other securities take place. Trading activity is overseen by the National Association of Securities Dealers (NASD).

— P —

Participant Contributions

The money that employees contribute to their 401k plan/defined contribution plan.

Participant-Directed Investing

When the employee decides how to invest his or her funds. It is the company's responsibility to offer a variety of investment opportunities so that the employee can make investments according to his or her long term goals and risk.

PBGC

The Pension Benefit Guarantee Corp. The PBGC is a guarantee fund established by ERISA which covers all defined benefit pension plans. Companies with a defined benefit plan must pay premiums into this fund according to the number of employees in the plan and the current ratio of assets to liabilities in the plan.

Plan

The term "Plan" means "retirement plan," which can be a 401(k) Plan, a Profit Sharing Plan, or a Pension Plan. These plans are known as "qualified" retirement plans. They are employer-sponsored plans that, under the Internal Revenue Code Section 401, receive favorable tax treatment. There are only two types of "qualified" retirement plans: Defined Contribution Plans and Defined Benefit Plans.

Other retirement savings plans for small businesses are called SEPs, and SIMPLE's. These plans are for small businesses and can be less complicated and less expensive than a 401(k). They also have less flexibility and generally lower limits for savings.

Plan Document

A document approximately 100 pages in length describing the terms of a qualified retirement plan, such as a 401(k) plan or pension plan. The plan document must be maintained by the adopting employer in accordance with the laws set forth by Congress and the rules and regulations prescribed by the IRS and DOL.

Portfolio

The group of individual securities held by a person or an Institution, such as a mutual fund or collective trust.

Price-Earnings Ratio (P/E)

Market price per share divided by the firm's earnings per share. A measure of how the market currently values the firm's earnings growth and risk prospects.

Price-to-Book Ratio

Market price per share divided by book value (tangible assets less all liabilities) per share. A measure of stock valuation relative to net assets. A high ratio might imply an overvalued situation; a low ratio might indicate an overlooked stock.

Principal

The original amount of money invested or lent, as distinguished from profits or interest earned on that money.

Profit Margin

Net earnings after taxes divided by sales. Measures the ability of a firm to generate earnings from sales.

Profit Sharing Plan

A defined contribution plan that uses a discretionary level of contributions as determined annually by the employer. Contributions do not have to be based on profits.

Program Trading

In "Program Trading," computer-based trigger points are established in which large volume trades are indicated. The technique is used by institutional investors.

Prohibited Transaction

When you engage in a prohibited transaction, it is considered self-dealing. Parties in interest (the plan sponsor or employer, plan participant, trustee, and plan advisors) cannot benefit from the following actions: 1. the sale, exchange or leasing of property, 2. the lending of money or extension of credit, 3. the furnishing of goods, services or facilities, 4. the transfer to, or use by, for the benefit of, the income or assets of the plan, 5. any act that deals with the plan asset's or income for the benefit of the fiduciary, 6. the receipt by the fiduciary of any consideration for the fiduciary's own personal account from any party dealing with the plan in connection with the income or assets of the plan. (This is why fiduciary advisors relinquish their brokerage licenses and are fee only).

Prospectus

The written statement that discloses the terms of a securities offering or a mutual fund. Strict rules govern the information that must be disclosed to investors in the prospectus. You should always read the prospectus on any mutual fund before investing.

Provider

An organization (such as an insurance company, mutual fund group, bank/ trust company or third party administrator) that offers retirement plan services.

Prudent Investor Rule

The rule for evaluating fiduciary prudence. The most recent rule (set forth in 1992) differs from the traditional Prudent Man Rule in that it indicates that: (1) no asset is automatically imprudent but must be suitable to the needs of the beneficiaries, (2) the entire portfolio is viewed when evaluating the prudence of a fiduciary, and (3) certain actions can be delegated to other agents and fiduciaries. ERISA Sec. 404(a)(1)(C) generally follows the approach of the Prudent Investor Rule.

Prudent Man Rule

A rule originally stated in 1830 by the Supreme Judicial Court of Massachusetts in Harvard College v. Amory (9 Pick. [Mass.] 446) that, in investing, all that can be required of a trustee is that he conduct himself faithfully and exercise a sound discretion and observe how men of prudence, discretion, and intelligence manage their own affairs not in regard to speculation, but in regard to the permanent disposition of their funds considering the probable income as well as the probable safety of the capital to be invested. The current (1959) model uniform rule categorizes certain types of assets as automatically imprudent, looks at each investment separately in determining prudence, and prohibits the delegation of responsibilities. Most states have adopted the Rule as a part of state fiduciary law, usually with certain different specifics from state to state.

Put Option

The right to sell stock at a specified (exercise) price within a specified period of time.

—Q—

Qualified Default Investment Alternative (QDIA)

A QDIA involves a participant in an individual account plan such as a 401(k) plan. If a plan participant does not submit investment instructions to the plan administrator, the participant is treated as if he or she exercised actual control over the assets in their account. The employer will invest the money in a qualified default investment (QDI): a life-cycle fund or targeted-to-retirement fund, a balanced account or a managed account. The employer retains no fiduciary liability for a QDIA provided they give proper participant notice and satisfy the five requirements listed below.

QDIA Requirements

1 The investment alternative must not hold or permit the acquisition of employer securities unless under a mutual fund or for managed arrangements holding employer matching contributions.

2 There can be no penalties imposed to transfer to an alternative investment.

3 A QDIA must be managed by an investment manager as defined in Sec 3(38) of ERISA or by an investment company registered under the Investment Company Act of 1940.

4 A QDIA must be diversified so as to minimize the risk of large losses.

5 The QDIA must constitute one of the three types of investment products previously described.

Qualified Plan

A retirement plan that meets the rules and regulations of the Dept of Labor and Internal Revenue Service. Contributions to a plan are tax-deductible and the earnings on the contributions are tax-deferred until withdrawn.

— R —

Real Rate of Return

The annual percentage return realized on an investment, adjusted for changes in the price level due to inflation or deflation.

Relative Strength

Price performance of a stock divided by the price performance of an appropriate index over the same time period. A measure of price trends that indicate how a stock is performing relative to other stocks or mutual funds.

Return

Consists of income plus capital gains (or losses) relative to the investment.

Risk/Return Trade-off

The balance an investor must decide on between the desire for low risk and high returns, since low levels of uncertainty (low risk) are associated with low potential returns and high levels of uncertainty (high risk) are associated with high potential returns.

Risk

Possibility that an investment's actual return will be different than expected, including the possibility of losing some or all of the original investment.

Measured by variability of historical returns or dispersion of historical returns around their average return.

Rolling Information Ratio

This is a risk-adjusted performance measurement. It measures the value added or subtracted by the manager per unit of risk.

Rolling Performance Consistency

The total returns of the funds, using rolling periods to minimize the end period dominance of recent performance history and to provide more comprehensive performance data to evaluate.

Rolling Selection Return

Each fund's returns will be compared to the market benchmarks of various investment styles to determine the custom portfolio benchmark that best explains the pattern and consistency of each Fund's returns. The Investment Fiduciary will then compare each fund's performance to its custom portfolio benchmark to determine the value added or subtracted by its manager.

Rollover

An employee's transfer of retirement funds from one retirement plan to another plan of the same type or to an IRA without incurring a tax liability. The transfer must be made within 60 days of receiving a cash distribution. The law requires 20 percent federal income tax withholding on money eligible for rollover if it is not moved directly to the second plan or an investment company.

Roth 401(k)

A provision in the Plan Document allowing plan participants to invest their money after tax. Roth 401(k) money, if held in the plan for five years, can be withdrawn after age 59 ½ tax free.

— S —

Salary Reduction Plan (Cash or Deferred Arrangement)

A Cash or Deferred Arrangement is a defined contribution plan that allows participants to have a portion of their compensation (otherwise payable in cash) contributed pre-tax to a retirement account on their behalf. Common names for Cash or Deferred Plans (named after the section of the Internal Revenue Code that establishes the rules for the plan) are 401(k), 403(b) and 457. These plans are also referred to as "defined contribution" plans.

Savings or Thrift Plan

A defined contribution plan in which participants make contributions on a discretionary basis and to which employers may also contribute. Contributions are made with after-tax earnings.

Sharpe Ratio

A risk-adjusted measure calculated by using standard deviation and excess return to determine reward per unit of risk. The higher the Sharpe Ratio the better the funds historical risk-adjusted performance. It can be used to compare two funds on how much excess return each fund achieved for a certain level of risk.

Soft Dollars

The purchase of research materials from brokerage firms and paid for by commissions (or part of the commissions) generated by securities transactions of trust accounts. Covered by Section 28(e)(1) of the Securities Exchange Act of 1934.

SPD

The Summary Plan Description (SPD) summarizes your retirement plan and tells you what the plan provides and how it operates.

Standard & Poor's 500 Index

An index of 500 major U.S. corporations. It is a broad-based measurement of changes in stock market conditions based on the average performance of 500 of the largest companies in the U.S. The index tracks industrial, transportation, financial, and utility stocks.

Stock Dividend

A dividend paid in additional shares of stock rather than in cash.

Stock Split

Dividing a company's existing stock into more shares. For example, in a 2-for-1 split, each stockholder would receive an additional share for each share formerly held and the price of each share would be half of the original share.

Stockbroker

An agent referred to a registered representative who, for a commission, handles orders to buy and sell securities.

Stop-limit Order

An order placed with a broker to buy or sell at a specified price or better after a given stop price has been reached or passed.

Stop-loss Order

An order placed with a broker to buy or sell when a certain price is reached; designed to limit an investor's loss on a security position.

Summary Annual Report

This summarizes the annual financial reports that plans are required to file with the government.

Summary Plan Description

See SPD.

— T —

Tax Free Rollover

A provision whereby an individual receiving a lump sum distribution from a qualified pension or profit sharing plan can preserve the tax deferred status of these funds by a "rollover" into an IRA or another qualified plan if rolled over within sixty days of receipt. (See "Rollover" in the Glossary above.)

Top Heavy Plan

A plan whose account balances of key employees exceed 60% of the total account balances.

Trailing Performance

The investment performance of the funds evaluated using weighted trailing annualized total returns.

Transaction Costs

Costs incurred buying or selling securities. These include brokers' commissions and dealers' spreads (the difference between the price the dealer paid for a security and for which he can sell it).

Treasury Bill

A short-term debt security issued by the federal government for periods of one year or less.

Treasury Bond

A longer-term debt security issued by the federal government for a period of seven years or longer.

Treasury Note

A longer-term debt security issued by the federal government for a period of one to seven years.

12(b)1 Fees

A plan that permits a fund to pay some or all of the costs of distributing its shares to the public. Some of these plans provide for payment of specific expenses, such as advertising, sales literature and dealer incentives. Both load and no-load funds may adopt 12(b)1 plans. There are not hidden charges but are clearly explained in the fund's prospectus. The majority of such plans have maximum annual charges of 0.25% (one quarter of 1%). 12(b)1 charges are included in the total expense ratio figures which are provided in a fund's literature.

Trust

A fiduciary relationship in which one person (the trustee) is the holder of the legal title to property (the trust property) subject to an equitable obligation (an obligation enforceable in a court of equity) to keep or use the property for the benefit of another person (the beneficiary).

Trustee
> The person(s) or entity with the authority and discretion over the management and control of plan assets.

Turnover
> The rate at which securities in a portfolio or mutual fund are replaced, on average, in the portfolio or fund.

— U —

Unfunded Vested Pension Liability
> In a defined benefit pension plan, the difference between the value of the vested (non-forfeitable) benefits under the plan and the market value of the plan's assets.

Unfunded Prior Service Pension Liability
> In a defined benefit pension plan, the difference between the value of the projected future benefit costs and the unamortized portion of prior benefit costs under the plan and the market value of the plan's assets.

— V —

Valuation
> Valuing an asset to determine it current worth.

Value Line index
> The index represents 1,700 companies from the New York and American Stock Exchanges and the over-the-counter market. It is an equal-weighted index, which means each of the 1,700 stocks, regardless of market price or total market value, are weighted equally.

Vesting
> The period of time an employee must work at a firm before gaining access to employer-contributed funds or benefit. For 401(k) plans, employee contributions are immediately vested, but employer contributions may be vested over a period of several years.

— W —

Wrap Account

A special type of brokerage arrangement where the investor places their funds and pays an annual fee for investment management services. All costs are "wrapped" into this one fee, including all administrative fees, commission costs, management fees.

— Y —

Yield Curve

A curve that shows interest rates at a specific point for all bonds having equal risk but different maturity dates. Usually, government bonds are used to construct such curves.

Yield to Maturity

The rate of return anticipated on a bond if it is held until its maturity date.

Yield

The amount of interest paid on a bond divided by the price. It is the measure of income generated by a bond. (The yield is not the total return measure because it does not include capital gains or losses.)

— Z —

Zero Coupon Bond

A bond bought at a discount to its face value that does not pay interest, but rather pays face value on maturity. The longer the time between when you purchased the bond and when it matures, the deeper the discount. Your earnings are the difference between your purchase price (the discount) and the face value at maturity.

ISBN 142513604-4